MANAGING MEANING IN UKRAINE

Information Policy Series

Edited by Sandra Braman

The Information Policy series publishes research on and analysis of significant problems in the field of information policy, including decisions and practices that enable or constrain information, communication, and culture irrespective of the legal siloes in which they have traditionally been located as well as state-law-society interactions. Defining information policy as all laws, regulations, and decision-making principles that affect any form of information creation, processing, flows, and use, the series includes attention to the formal decisions, decision-making processes, and entities of government; the formal and informal decisions, decision-making processes, and entities of private- and public-sector agents capable of constitutive effects on the nature of society; and the cultural habits and predispositions of governmentality that support and sustain government and governance. The parametric functions of information policy at the boundaries of social, informational, and technological systems are of global importance because they provide the context for all communications, interactions, and social processes.

A complete list of the books in the Information Policy series appears at the back of this book.

MANAGING MEANING IN UKRAINE

INFORMATION, COMMUNICATION, AND NARRATION SINCE THE EUROMAIDAN REVOLUTION

GÖRAN BOLIN AND PER STÅHLBERG

The MIT Press
Cambridge, Massachusetts
London, England

The MIT Press would like to thank the anonymous peer reviewers who provided comments on drafts of this book. The generous work of academic experts is essential for establishing the authority and quality of our publications. We acknowledge with gratitude the contributions of these otherwise uncredited readers.

This book was set in Bembo Book MT Pro by Westchester Publishing Services. Printed and bound in the United States of America.

Library of Congress Cataloging-in-Publication Data

Names: Bolin, Göran, author. | Ståhlberg, Per, author.
Title: Managing meaning in Ukraine : information, communication, and
    narration since the Euromaidan revolution / Göran Bolin and Per
    Ståhlberg.
Description: Cambridge, Massachusetts : The MIT Press, [2023] | Series:
    Information policy | Includes bibliographical references and index.
Identifiers: LCCN 2022033259 (print) | LCCN 2022033260 (ebook) |
    ISBN 9780262545563 (paperback) | ISBN 9780262374583 (epub) |
    ISBN 9780262374576 (pdf)
Subjects: LCSH: Mass media—Ukraine. | Meaning (Philosophy) | Information
    policy—Ukraine. | Narration (Rhetoric)—Social aspects—Ukraine. | Mass
    media and culture—Ukraine. | Ukraine Conflict, 2014—Mass media and
    the war. | Ukraine—History—Euromaidan Protests, 2013-2014—Influence.
Classification: LCC P92.U38 B65 2023 (print) | LCC P92.U38 (ebook) |
    DDC 302.2309477/09051—dc23/eng/20221206
LC record available at https://lccn.loc.gov/2022033259
LC ebook record available at https://lccn.loc.gov/2022033260

10 9 8 7 6 5 4 3 2 1

CONTENTS

Stuart Hall, the great Jamaican-born theorist of communication and culture, told a delicious story about what happened when he finally received an invitation to deliver a guest lecture at Oxford University. He opened by describing what it was like to come from the margins and then asked who in the audience came from the economic, social, and political elites with which the institution had always been associated. No one raised a hand, although one person confessed afterward that he had been embarrassed to admit his background in public. "When I got to the center," reported Hall, "no one was there."

As we learn in *Managing Meaning in Ukraine*, the same can be said of at least some versions of the informational state—the kind of state that specializes in the use of informational power rather than power in its instrumental, structural, or symbolic ("soft") forms. Bolin and Ståhlberg's analysis of Ukrainian information policy from 2013 to just before the Russian invasion in 2022 finds that it was not driven by the state, as policy analysts typically assume. Instead, it was driven first by private-sector entities interested in creating new markets for their communication products and then by international forces that provided direction and funding for small local groups that were shape-shifting and multifaceted. The combined effect was a perceived Ukrainian state that, in reality, neither was driven by the state nor had a center. With this insight, Bolin and Ståhlberg importantly move forward our understanding of the informational state, pointing out that there is more than one kind and presenting the challenge to identify others. Bernard Silberman's 1993 book *Cages of Reason* undertook this task for the bureaucratic state, showing that, informationally, France, Japan, the United States, and Great Britain operated very differently, even though all were categorized as having the same form of government.

This is not the only significant theoretical and conceptual contribution of *Managing Meaning in Ukraine*. Scholars and practitioners typically refer to public diplomacy and related information policy as information management. These authors argue that it is the management of meaning that is really at stake—sense-making by those who receive messages, not the intentions of senders and/or the information sent. Those analyzing or involved in strategic communication talk about producing narratives, the telling of stories that unfold sequentially over time and involve causal relations. The reality, as Bolin and Ståhlberg point out, is that only fragments are circulated, incomplete narrative elements and snippets of heterogeneous information that the authors valuably refer to as *preforms* of narrative. These elements can be formed into assemblages in multiple ways that continue to change as they are mediated and remediated. Memes are examples, but fragments need not reach the meme level of common usage to be utilized as communicative resources. Multiple literatures have long distinguished between information and knowledge, or information and narrative. Today, these fragmentary preforms of narrative add a third, necessary category to all such distinctions.

Research and thinking on public opinion and persuasion have focused on reception, or what Stuart Hall refers to as the decoding phase of communication processes. To understand the creation, distribution, and effects of preforms of narrative, though, Bolin and Ståhlberg argue that Hall's concept of encoding—how messages come into being as meaningful assemblages—must receive the same kind of analytical attention. When Hall first introduced his ideas about encoding and decoding in the early 1970s, he was talking about the mass media, with a particular interest in television. The authors of this book take the position that the concepts are still valid today but need further development because the environment has changed qualitatively in terms of who is producing content, what media they use to distribute it, the number of points at which messages are remediated, and the number of directions in which messages flow.

Encoding takes place through the circulation of an ever-growing archive of image and text fragments. In their analysis of encoding, Bolin and Ståhlberg make three additional conceptual moves, two involving technologies and the third involving people. Going beyond the somewhat celebratory depiction of users who take part in remediation processes as involved in prosumption—the simultaneous production and consumption of content—they remind us how such practices serve the marketing and promotional activities of big capital and traditional mass media productions. They also extend our vision beyond content manipulation and distribution to include presentation technologies that have an impact on the nature of the content circulating today. Tools such as PowerPoint, the authors point out, make it easy to take fragments out of texts for other uses—or to replace texts altogether, as slide decks may be all we have. As the authors put it, presentation media "play with discursive elements and narrative components without producing any stable or unified story that reaches narrative closure . . . [it] is a technology that offers assemblages of meaning rather than narratives." On the human side, the book highlights the fluidity of roles, industry affiliations, and sector identities among those active in the effort to develop and promote Ukraine as a recognizable state with particular features. The industries are standard—public relations, marketing, journalism, fact-checking, public policy, and so on—but which individuals and organizations are doing what keeps changing.

Managing Meaning in Ukraine is a book for many audiences. Since Russia's 2022 invasion, Ukraine has "hardened" as a state, as any entity would in response to threats to its survival and explicit conflicts over its borders. It now has a center, although private-sector and voluntary activities of multiple types—by both domestic and international actors—remain important. Anyone seeking to understand what happened between Ukraine and Russia in 2022, which grew out of so much that happened before, will find this book essential reading. The case of Ukraine is key, as it is already apparent that these developments are pivotal to struggles over a global reorientation of power. This analysis contributes to our understanding of the evolution of all transitional states and pushes us to appreciate differences among informational states. From an international relations perspective, this history of the transformation of nation branding into public diplomacy into national information policy into information warfare offers profound insights.

The value of Bolin and Ståhlberg's work goes even further, with theoretical and conceptual innovations that open up a number of research agendas for the many fields involved. We are not all Ukrainians, but we all live in the communication world the authors have made so visible.

ACKNOWLEDGMENTS

This is not the book we imagined we would write when we embarked on our joint academic journey a little more than a decade ago. We both had an interest in questions of nation, nationalism, branding, and popular culture. Our interest then was how popular culture—or culture more generally—was hijacked as a means to achieve other ends, most of which were commercial or political. In a way, you could say that this particular research topic came to us, rather than the other way around. We believe, however, that this serendipity has led us to regard our present object of inquiry—far outside our "comfort zone," as today's parlance would put it—from a somewhat different perspective. We hope readers of this book will also be confronted with a different set of concepts and terminology and perhaps a different way of approaching societal matters.

It is somewhat trite to say that a book is the product of more people than the two authors credited on the cover. But such statements become hackneyed because there is some truth to them. We were fortunate to have the support of funding institutions such as the Foundation for Baltic and East European Studies, which generously funded the two projects on which this book is based: Nation Branding: The Nation as Community and Commodity in Eastern Europe (2012–2015) and Propaganda and Management of Information in the Ukraine-Russia Conflict: From Nation Branding to Information War (2015–2018). We also benefited from seminars and workshops funded by the Centre for Baltic and East European Studies (CBEES) at Södertörn University, as well as support from our colleagues in the university's Department of Media and Communication Studies. We received some stimulating feedback from students enrolled in the master's course on nation branding we taught jointly between 2015 and 2017, especially Karin Hallgren, Kateryna Boyko, Iryna Holovko, and Giulia Santori. Karin, Iryna, and Giulia took part in fieldwork during the Eurovision Song Contest held in Kyiv in May 2017, helping us gather empirical data and discussing these data with us. Iryna also helped us with organizational tasks as well as translation during and after the fieldwork, and Kateryna provided valuable comments on the manuscript. The course benefited greatly from guest lectures by Katja Valaskivi, Nadia Kaneva, and Galina Miazhevich, with whom we have collaborated over the years.

We also received tremendous help from the three postdoctoral researchers involved in the two previously mentioned projects. Paul Jordan worked with us on the nation branding project, and his background in eastern European studies and enormous knowledge of the Eurovision Song Contest were invaluable. Having already done research on Ukrainian branding, Paul was instrumental in connecting us with key informants in Kyiv during the initial phases of the project. Yuliya Yurchuk and Liudmila Voronova worked with us on the information war project. Yuliya, a native Ukrainian and a historian by training, broadened our understanding of Ukrainian culture and society. As a native Russian, Liudmila provided the same insights into Russian culture, with a specific focus on journalistic practices. Both were energetic fieldworkers who contributed to amassing interview material and other empirical data for the project.

We would also like to extend thanks to two of our departmental colleagues. Fredrik Stiernstedt took part in the fieldwork for the Eurovision Song Contest in Kyiv. Roman Horbyk has been a valuable discussion partner, translator, and field guide over the years. Roman's vast network of contacts helped us track down empirical material, backtrack and map the Euromaidan events, and provide context to the Ukrainian media landscape.

We presented early versions of our work at various international conferences: the International Communication Association (ICA) conferences in Chicago, Fukuoka, San Diego, and Washington; the European Communication Research and Education Association (ECREA) conference in Prague; and the European Association of Social Anthropologists (EASA) conference in Stockholm. We also presented parts of our analysis at workshops and seminars at Universidade Católica Portuguesa, Universidade Nova de Lisboa, Tampere University, Aarhus University, Loughborough University, the Institute of Russian and Eurasian Studies at Uppsala University, and the Centre for Baltic and East European Studies at Södertörn University. We wish to extend a collective thanks to all those who arranged these occasions and to the participants who commented on and challenged our propositions.

Of tremendous importance was our presentation at the Workshop Series for Information Policy arranged by Sandra Braman in May 2021. We benefited greatly from comments on drafts of the first two chapters. The workshop series also proved to be an excellent initiative for bringing our thoughts about information policy—in the widest sense of the term—together. We were enriched by discussions of other works in progress at these workshops. We applaud this interdisciplinary initiative and hope we contributed to a deepening of the discussion around policy and related matters. We also owe special thanks to Sandra for encouraging us to publish our work in the context of information policy in the first place. We would like to think that this tweaking of our initial points of departure made our discussion more original than it would have been otherwise. Whether this is the case is, of course, up to the reader to judge.

Two Ukrainian universities offered opportunities for academic encounters. The Journalism Department at the National University of Kyiv-Mohyla Academy welcomed us on almost every visit to Kyiv. In particular, Professor Yevhen Fedchenko provided invaluable insights into the field of fact-checking in Ukraine. At Taras Shevchenko National University, also in Kyiv, we had a chance to both engage with scholars and lecture to students.

Last but not least, we are incredibly indebted to our informants in Kyiv. A lot of people working in government offices, public relations companies, news agencies and outlets, and civil society organizations took the time to share information and ideas with us during extended and often repeated meetings. Many of these public individuals are named in the chapters that follow. Others, too numerous to mention, should know that we are tremendously grateful for their contributions.

Göran Bolin and Per Ståhlberg

INTRODUCTION

On the morning of 24 February 2022, Russia launched a full-scale invasion of Ukraine, attacking the country from several directions. The war, however, had started eight years earlier, in 2014, with Russia's annexation of the Crimean Peninsula on the Black Sea. But what had previously been a low-scale, regionally delimited war suddenly escalated to unthinkable dimensions. This book is concerned with events preceding the full-scale assault on Ukraine. The manuscript had been completed when Russian bombs started to fall on cities across the country, and the outcome of the war is still unknown as the final version of the book goes to press. Except for minor adjustments, we have not rewritten the study to acknowledge the most recent atrocities. Still, we are very much aware that this book will be framed by the context of the war, whatever direction it takes. And so it should. We believe the eight years preceding the 2022 Russian invasion are crucial for understanding the war, especially its communicative dimensions. Our initial impressions from the first few weeks of the war strengthened this belief, and as we watched the videos, images, and other communicative efforts produced in Ukraine and disseminated to the world, we could see that they were the results of a longer period of development among those who manage meaning in Ukraine. For the Ukrainians, the assaults that shook the world were not unexpected. This book is about Ukrainian preparations for a worst-case scenario, the fruits of which can now be watched on screens all over the world.

The period we are studying evolved in discrete phases. First, we examine communicative activities during 2013, just before there was any fear of war. Second, we refer to the three months of the Euromaidan Revolution in the winter of 2013–2014. Most of the book, however, is concerned with the long period of low-scale war and related information management from the Russian annexation of Crimea in 2014 to 2021, the year before the full-scale invasion. With the brutal escalation in 2022, a new phase of history started for Ukraine, in many respects with completely different characteristics. However, nothing grows out of a void.

Theoretically, the book raises questions about communicative action in Ukraine and related to the country's specific situation since 2013. The wider context also concerns general developments since the collapse of the Soviet Union and how Ukraine has related to the Russian sphere of interest. How is it possible to organize information policy in times of deep national crisis? What roles do governmental, corporate, and civil society actors play in times of revolution when the state is in turmoil? How do these domestic actors respond to external aggression and propaganda? With the dramatic escalation of the situation in Ukraine, these questions have increased in relevance.

UKRAINE: IN SEARCH OF A NEW FACE

When we first decided to study communication practices in Ukraine, there was no war with Russia. It was early 2013, and we were interested in how government authorities in cooperation with public relations (PR) consultancies and the corporate business sector were trying to promote a favorable image of Ukraine to an international audience. Such nation branding campaigns have been widespread since the 1990s, not least in eastern Europe, where the end of the Cold War encouraged many states to rid themselves of their immediate Soviet past and show the rest of the world a new face. We chose Ukraine not because it had been particularly successful in its nation branding efforts. It fact, the opposite was true. Ukraine had launched several branding campaigns, but none of them had been notable, and Ukraine was rarely, if ever, mentioned in the field of nation branding research.

Ukraine is geographically the largest European country, and with about 45 million inhabitants, it is the most populous of the post-Soviet states in eastern Europe.[1] Despite its size, Ukraine was fairly anonymous compared with its neighbor Poland or the Baltic states. Like a number of other post-Soviet countries, Ukraine has a very short history of sovereignty. Although it enjoyed a brief period of independence after World War I as the Ukrainian People's Republic (1917–1921), modern independence came with the collapse of the Soviet Union in 1991 (Wolczuk 2000). Since the fall of the Soviet Union, Ukraine had balanced on the border between the European Union and the Russian sphere of influence. Gradually, however, Ukraine started to build closer ties with the EU, and an association agreement between Ukraine and the EU was supposed to be signed on 28 November 2013. We expected that established forms of nation branding practices could be rather difficult to implement in Ukraine.

Our first field trip to Kyiv took place in May 2013, with the aim of building contacts with public servants at government departments and marketing professionals in the PR industry who had been involved in previous nation branding campaigns. The government had commissioned some of these efforts, and private corporations had initiated others. The latest campaign had been conducted in cooperation with international broadcasters such as BBC World and CNN, just before the 2012 European Soccer Championship cohosted by Ukraine and Poland. In the local PR business in Kyiv, the commercial field of place branding (promoting cities, regions, or the country as a whole) was small, and it was easy to identify the bureaus and individuals involved in previous campaigns.

The marketing business in Kyiv was not large, and it soon became apparent that all the major players knew one another. As in all social fields, the relationship between actors can be described as both collaborative and competitive. Among branding consultants, one could also sense a notion of reflexivity and self-criticism. Several of the earlier campaigns had been met with harsh domestic criticism concerning both their content and the questionable use of public money. In fact, even those who had participated in these campaigns to improve Ukraine's international image regarded them as failures. Often, however, they blamed the government for a lack of proper coordination. They also expressed a sense of urgency—a sense of being at a crossroads. This concern was present among PR consultants and politicians but also in the media: Ukraine was perceived as almost invisible to the rest of the world and in need of a recognizable "face" (Ståhlberg and Bolin 2016). An article in the English-language magazine *Kyiv Weekly* stated that "the average European cannot imagine a Ukrainian because they have never seen one." Or if they could imagine one, the author explained, it would be "a negative image of a 'nation of bandits, prostitutes and migrant workers'" (Kabachiy 2013, 2).

At the time, we were definitely part of that ignorant foreign audience. Neither of us had visited Ukraine before, and our knowledge of the country was not much better than that of the average European. We were familiar with the names of the larger cities and some major events from recent history, such as the Orange Revolution in 2004 and the singer Ruslana's victory in the Eurovision Song Contest the same year. And we remembered

Yulia Tymoshenko, one of the leaders who became an iconic face of the revolution. But beyond that, we knew very little. Chernobyl was mainly a frightening metonym for human technological disaster, and if we associated it with any particular country, it was the Soviet Union. Most people in Sweden, our home country, would probably be unable to accurately locate this nuclear catastrophe in today's Ukraine. The same is true of the city of Poltava, which, as every Swedish primary school pupil knows, is where Swedish king Charles XII lost a battle against the Russian tsar in 1709. (It probably evokes the same connotations for Swedes as Waterloo does for French citizens.) Few Swedes would place Poltava in Ukraine, indicating that the worries of the Ukrainian branders were justified.

The people we met on our first visit to Kyiv were arguably not representative of the average Ukrainian citizen. They were professionals working in the PR industry, in government departments, or in the journalistic media. Most were fluent in English, and many had been educated at UK or US universities. They were clearly oriented to the West and were strongly convinced that Ukraine needed to move closer to Europe and the EU. In their minds, the main problem was that Ukraine was too close to Russian culture and values. When they talked about branding Ukraine, the implied audience was in the West, and they had great expectations for the upcoming association agreement with the EU. There were also ponderings about the new nation branding campaign commissioned by the Ministry of Tourism.

We returned to Kyiv to see the presentation of that new campaign, which was to be launched at the Second Kyiv International Tourism Forum on 10– 12 October. The first day's events took place at the Club of the Cabinet of Ministers of Ukraine and was opened by the vice prime minister of Ukraine, Oleksandr Vilkul; the program included a number of domestic dignitaries, foreign diplomats, and representatives of the EU, UNESCO, and the World Tourism Organization. Talks were simultaneously translated into English, Ukrainian, and Russian. At the forum, Vilkul announced a new strategy to brand Ukraine as an international tourist destination. The ambitious goal was for it to become one of the ten leading countries in world tourism.

The opening ceremony was followed by a session where the new tourism campaign was presented. The contract for orchestrating this campaign had been won by WikiCitiNomika, a PR firm with previous experience in city branding in Ukraine. During the development of the campaign, it cooperated closely with the German agency GIZ (German Association of

International Cooperation), and WikiCitiNomika presented the campaign strategies and graphic design components together with the German ambassador to Ukraine and the local director of GIZ. The central message was that Ukraine was a country of cultural contrasts coexisting in peace. Ukraine was both East and West, Orthodox Christianity and Catholicism, tradition and modernity, and so on. Graphically, this message was expressed with the letter *U* (for Ukraine), in which the font heights represented a binary contrast that, when conjoined, made a happy smile.

The second day was organized quite differently from the first day's opening speeches and presentations. The main Ukrainian tourist attractions were displayed in an exhibition at the Ukrainian House—a huge Soviet-style building near Maidan Nezalezhnosti (Independence Square) in the center of the city. Around the exhibition were demonstrations and displays of the cultural heritages of Ukraine: traditional music, folk costumes, and works of art. The artwork included Petrykivka ornamental paintings, a style originating in the village of the same name in Dnipropetrovsk Oblast, for which Ukraine was applying to UNESCO for the status of intangible cultural heritage (later granted).

In addition to the displays of cultural heritage and commercial commodities, there was an exhibition booth for the promotion of EuroBasket 2015, which would take place in Kyiv, and another booth related to Ukraine's ambitions to host the Winter Olympic Games in 2022. Coming from Scandinavia, and not speaking either Ukrainian or Russian, we soon realized we did not belong to the primary target audience. There was very little information in English, and most of the commercial exhibitors addressed their displays of tourist destinations, facilities, and commodities to a Russian-speaking audience. As we had learned from the vice prime minister's PowerPoint slides the day before, tourism in Ukraine still meant visitors from Russia and other neighboring countries. The slides themselves were in Russian, and many of the guests came from former Soviet countries. However, as we walked around the displays, talked with exhibitors, and listened in on seminars, it was evident that many people had high hopes for an expanded tourist market.

Only a few weeks later, all these expectations were radically erased. At the last minute, President Viktor Yanukovych backed out of the association agreement with the EU in the hopes of building tighter trade agreements with Russia. A few postings on Facebook led to demonstrations at Maidan Nezalezhnosti, and the square was soon known internationally as Euromaidan.

The protests escalated rapidly and were followed by a violent crackdown by the police and special riot forces (Berkut). By February 2014, more than one hundred people had been killed.

Paradoxically, the clashes between protesters and police in Kyiv meant that Ukraine no longer needed a branding campaign to get international attention. Just like many other European citizens and other news consumers around the world, we followed the events closely on international and national broadcast news channels, as well as on Twitter and Facebook. The violence in Kyiv and other cities in Ukraine continued until late February 2014, when the president fled the country. This was followed shortly thereafter by Russian aggression, including the annexation of Crimea in March and a Russia-backed "separatist" war in the regions of Donetsk and Luhansk. Most sensational was the downing of Malaysian passenger flight MH17 over eastern Ukraine in July, killing all 298 passengers and crew.

Managing the domestic information around these events was a challenge for the government, which was quite weak at the time. And if it was difficult to control the flow of information domestically, it was even more difficult to do so internationally. The war has continued since then and escalated in February 2022, providing a continuous flow of news stories in the international media.

A NEW INFORMATION LANDSCAPE

The events following the Euromaidan Revolution brought us back to what was once a classic concern of media research: war and propaganda. Ukraine ended up in a situation that was increasingly understood as an information war with Russia, and scholars were soon paying attention to these events, which were increasingly framed in terms of propaganda, iWar, or hybrid warfare.[2] By far, the Russian side of this discursive conflict has received the most attention, both in news reporting and in research. The dominant perception was that Russia (often metonymically expressed as "Putin" or "the Kremlin") was acting in an extremely well-organized and strategic way and making use of new communication technologies such as bots and social media manipulation (see Kuzio 2017). Furthermore, this development seemed to converge with a more general awareness of the communication patterns of populist regimes in various places around the world, their sometimes hostile way of relating to traditional media, and their relaxed distinctions between fact and fiction.

Concepts such as fake news and trolling—concepts with high rhetorical but little analytical value—became commonplace in discussions.

At this juncture, we became increasingly interested in other types of information policymaking besides nation branding. The communication situation in Ukraine also stood out as more interesting to us than Russia's activities. The way Ukraine managed its response to aggression and tried to control information flows was worth understanding: if there was a powerful, well-synchronized propaganda apparatus on the Russian side with the ability to disseminate a particularly biased image of the situation, how could Ukraine respond? What kind of counterimages could be produced, and by whom? In which forms and for which audiences?

Surprisingly, it soon became evident that the branding initiative in Kyiv was still alive. As one PR consultant stated, conflicts tend to blow over, while branding is long term. These professionals were biding their time until political conditions stabilized. However, more interesting from an information management perspective (Detlor 2010), several of our informants became deeply engaged in the Euromaidan protests and their aftermath, contributing their branding and communication skills to a number of initiatives with the explicit aim of responding to Russian propaganda.

This engagement was already apparent during those turbulent days in late November 2013. Notifications about the political situation started to appear on the Facebook and Twitter feeds of the PR consultants we had recently met. One of them was working at a PR bureau located a block from the Maidan, and he apparently went down to the square during his lunch break and photographed the crowd. From our interviews, it was clear that he had had great expectations about the EU agreement, but we were surprised that he joined the protests so soon and so openly. After all, nation branding professionals are highly dependent on their good relationships with state authorities, since they commission and pay for the campaigns. If the protests failed, these professionals would risk being out of business.

In the unstable situation that followed the ousting of President Yanukovych, an urgent need for information management was expressed. This was handled by private initiatives to provide foreign journalists with updated and reliable information about events in Ukraine. This was particularly critical when the situation escalated in 2014 and information started to appear from Russian sources offering their perspective. Much of the information being supplied to national and international news bureaus was from the eastern front, where the Ukraine army was fighting Russia-backed "separatists" in Donetsk and Luhansk. A group of PR professionals we knew set up the Ukraine Crisis Media Center (UCMC) in March 2014, with funding from a number of European and American organizations. The UCMC was launched with the aim of providing global media with "accurate and up-to-date information on the events in Ukraine."[3] From its location in the Hotel Ukraine, situated at the top of the Maidan, the UCMC offered news briefings and information support to foreign correspondents reporting from Ukraine.

The UCMC was not the only initiative undertaken during these turbulent days of the Euromaidan Revolution. Many other activists—both within the country and from the large Ukrainian diaspora—formed groups that engaged in communications activities geared toward both a national and an international audience. Many of these initiatives, such as Euromaidan Press, worked through Facebook and other online social media, disseminating the latest news from traditional trusted media sources as well as user-generated information. Activists supporting the regime change believed the Russian media deliberately interfered by spreading false information. To address this problem, a group of faculty and journalism students at the National University of Kyiv-Mohyla Academy launched StopFake to debunk stories from various sources that were spreading speculative or outright false information. They disseminated this information on a webpage and through social media. Simultaneously, a group of academic historians who had participated in the Euromaidan protests formed an initiative called Likbez to control how Ukraine's history was depicted in the media. As historians, however, their longer-term goal was to provide future generations of Ukrainians with history textbooks sanitized of a Russian bias (Yurchuk 2021).

A particularly noteworthy development in information management in Ukraine was the rapid launch of several new television channels that streamed continuous images from the Euromaidan Revolution. They provided many of the stock photos used by the international news media. Most successful was Hromadske TV, an initiative by young journalists in Kyiv that began broadcasting on the same day the demonstrations started. In fact, one of its reporters is thought to have instigated the protests by contacting friends on social media and telling them to gather at the square. Hromadske (Ukrainian for "public") was, however, not alone in streaming the protests live. We, too, switched between two other channels while following the dramatic events: UkrStream and Espreso TV.

As the war in eastern Ukraine became permanent, the Ukrainian government under new president Petro Poroshenko felt the need to implement a policy related to how information about the armed conflict was distributed both domestically and to an international audience. A new Ministry of Information Policy (MIP) was launched. This was not an uncontroversial decision. Critics feared that the Ukrainian government was trying to control and censor information—or perhaps fabricate lies—just like Russia. However, Ukraine did not have the kind of resources necessary to do so. The MIP was quite small, consisting of one minister and two deputy ministers, a few information officers (state secretaries), and administrative staff. In effect, the MIP relied on the cooperation of voluntary organizations engaged in communication projects related to the war (usually financed by donations and funds from foreign development organizations). However, at the MIP's disposal were the national news agency Ukrinform and the state television streaming channel UATV, both of which produce news information about Ukraine. Some of the state secretaries had backgrounds in PR and branding, and the MIP would eventually launch its own nation branding campaigns.

The Euromaidan events were intriguing and encouraged us to widen our research interest extensively. Our initial project about the branding of Ukraine had been confined to a limited number of actors involved in specific campaigns. The aggression from Russia stimulated several more civil society initiatives, ranging from fundraising and cultural performances to volunteer battalions fighting in the war. Particularly surprising was the amount of space available for private and voluntary initiatives. In this, we noted a similarity to the nation branding business: state and government authorities seemed to have less influence over communication projects than one would have expected, and information was managed by a plurality of civic and corporate actors contributing diverse experiences and skills. The chapters that follow describe and discuss the implications of this method of implementing information management and policy.

The developments in Ukraine after the Euromaidan Revolution actualized some classic themes of mass communication and media research, especially since the information management related to the Russian aggression was most often understood in terms of a propaganda war. Propaganda, however, is somewhat problematic as an analytical concept for pragmatic, ethical, and theoretical reasons. Pragmatically, few Ukrainian informants would consider their communicative activities to be propaganda. That may not be a complication for critical research conducted at some distance from the empirical world (the bulk of propaganda studies are also textual studies), but when interacting regularly with informants, the concept of propaganda is too negatively loaded. It is simply impossible to retain informants' trust if one calls the actions taken from the Ukrainian side propaganda. In common parlance (as well as in most but not all scholarly work), the concept has an entirely normative connotation. Propaganda is a practice of intentional deception that "others" engage in; it is definitely not something "we" do. Thus, the very use of the concept suggests a certain essentialist understanding of the studied phenomenon.

This brings up an ethical problem: it is dubious to discuss information and communication activities in "neutral" terms and then force the concept of propaganda on these activities in the analysis.

This circumstance is an apt illustration of the problem with propaganda as an analytical and theoretical concept: propaganda is usually understood as a form of communication that is orchestrated by a powerful propagandist (a state authority or political leader) to influence a target audience (of popular masses). Over time, its meaning has become more negative than it was in early research on mass communication. In their influential book *Propaganda and Persuasion*, Garth Jowett and Victoria O'Donnell define propaganda as "the deliberate, systematic attempt to shape perceptions, manipulate cognitions, and direct behaviour to achieve a response that furthers the desired intent of the propagandist" (1992, 2). It is only to a limited extent that such a definition would be helpful for making sense of communication activities in Ukraine.

Importantly, though, the word *propaganda* is relevant within the situations observed in Ukraine, and it is frequently used by the actors in this field (for that reason, the word appears on many of the following pages). All the communicative efforts we studied were framed by a strong conviction that Ukraine was threatened by propaganda—in much the same sense suggested by Jowett and O'Donnell's definition. Our informants insisted that there was a deliberate, systematic attempt to manipulate the whole world through false or biased information orchestrated by Russia or Russian interests. In that sense, propaganda is used in much the same way as the concept of fake news (Farkas and Schou 2020).

The intention of this book is neither to dispute that conviction nor to expose or critically examine Russian propaganda. Our scope is broader: this is a study of communicative practices by actors who are framing their efforts in relation to a threat they perceive as propaganda. Our interest is how that perception is articulated and acted on. Paraphrasing Clifford Geertz (who claimed that anthropologists are not studying villages but *in* villages), propaganda is "the locus of study [but] not the object of study" (1973, 22). We develop what this means theoretically for the analysis of information policy in Ukraine in the first chapter. In the remainder of this introduction, we present our aims and objectives and give an outline of the chapters to come.

CONTEXTS, AIMS, AND OUTLINE

This book describes and discusses the forms, agents, and platforms entangled in the complex political and communicative situation in Ukraine since 2013. The analysis is related to a specific historical context in which the combination of political tensions, commercial dynamics, and new communication technologies gives birth to novel forms of information management. A number of interested parties had a stake in the creation of Ukraine's information policy—governments and governmental administration (e.g., the MIP) and commercial actors, entrepreneurs, and activists—forming new alliances and cooperations.

This book focuses on Ukraine and the informational, political, social, and cultural conditions that are unique to the country. Importantly, this is *not* a book about the relations between Ukraine and Russia, nor is it about information wars (which is a problematic concept), although both these conditions are contextual to our analysis. There is plenty of research on Ukraine-Russia relations, as well as on information wars with a focus on these relations, but our fieldwork was exclusively about Ukraine and was carried out in that country. We sometimes reference work on international relations, but our focus is on how agents engage in information management and strive to manage meaning in communication practice, the communicative tools they take advantage of, and the consequences this has for narrative construction.

Ukraine is, at the time of this writing, the only European country involved in a war on its own territory. This is a truly extraordinary situation. This particularity aside, Ukraine is similar to other European countries in many respects, not least with its neighbors in eastern and central Europe. Ukraine has, for example, a strong presence of oligarchs, which means that there is a high degree of overlap between political and corporate power.[4] Ukraine has also scored high on corruption, like Bulgaria and other countries around the Black Sea.[5] As in these countries, Ukrainians have a very low level of trust in governmental institutions, including trust in politicians and the media.[6]

The strong oligarchy and its tight bonds to the Yanukovych government up until the Euromaidan events were also present in the realm of broadcast and print mass media. Five large media companies owned and dominated by five oligarchs controlled the media in Ukraine in what has been described as a system of "oligarch pluralism" (Horbyk et al. 2021, 42): Intermedia (Dmytro Firtash and Serhiy Lyovochkin), 1+1 Media (Ihor Kolomoyski), Media Group Ukraine (Rinat Akhmetov), StarLightMedia (Viktor Pinchuk), and Ukrainian Media Holding (Serhiy Kurchenko).[7] In addition to their broadcast and print media activities, all five media houses were active on websites, and 1+1 Media owned a news agency (Unian).[8] However friendly these five media holders were to the Yanukovych government in the years before Euromaidan, their loyalty quickly waned during the protests, and most of them reported Euromaidan events in a "balanced way, without pro-government or anti-opposition slant" (Szostek 2014, 9). As Joanna Szostek suggests, these oligarchs, many of whom had business interests in Europe, were "buying themselves insurance for the future" by acting neutral in a turbulent situation with an uncertain outcome (2014, 12).

It was significant that these oligarchs had a very strong hold on the broadcast media, since television was the dominant news provider for the Ukrainian population at the time. However, among younger segments of the population, internet news was more popular: 89 percent of fifteen- to twenty-four-year-olds and 73 percent of twenty-five- to thirty-four-year-olds reported that online news was their main source of information (Metzger and Tucker 2017, 175ff.). This meant that another context for the Euromaidan Revolution and the unfolding of events was the structure of the digital media landscape in Ukraine. In 2013 internet penetration was around 42 percent in Ukraine, which seems small compared with the European average of 68 percent (Onuch 2015a, 175). However, most of these users (82 percent) lived in urban areas, so the internet penetration in Kyiv was rather high (Metzger and Tucker 2017, 175ff.). And, taking into account that internet penetration among younger segments of the population was much higher, we can assume that those involved in the Euromaidan protests and their aftermath were highly connected.

The aim of this book is to analyze the management of meaning in Ukraine and to discuss how information policy is formed at the intersection of state politics, corporate business, and civil society activism.[9] In chapter 1 we account for our points of departure and our specific perspective on the management of meaning. We argue that information management and policy must be understood as stories or narratives told by a plurality of agents—journalists, PR professionals, political administrators, and many others. Notably, these stories are often constructed and take shape within networks of cooperating actors.

Narratives are also central to the professional practices surrounding nation branding, and through the construction of stories (narratives), branding and information policy converge. In the development of narratives, PR agencies and brand designers are searching for "success stories" they can use to attract tourists and foreign investments. Such language is also used in policy discussions among military advisers to governments.[10] But how are we to make sense of these narratives and counternarratives? What frameworks should we use to understand the complex communicative context in which information policy—broadly defined—in Ukraine is formed? In chapter 1 we also present our own model for understanding the management of information by focusing on the management of meaning through stories, narratives, images, and the like, and we relate this to previous literature on branding, propaganda, persuasion, and information management as well as to concepts such as nation branding, soft power, and public diplomacy. Our cultural approach to communication is grounded in the fact that before messages can have effects, they have to become *meaningful*, as British Jamaican cultural theorist Stuart Hall (1973) argues in one of his most cited works on the communication process. What appears meaningless to us will not affect us, as we largely disregard things that are incomprehensible. This is why stories— that is, messages organized within an intelligible narrative structure—are important. We understand the world around us through such stories. In this study we try to grasp how meaning is made during turbulent times.

We also discuss the consequences of various terminological choices, such as *propaganda* and *information war*, since the choice of terminology leads our thoughts in specific directions rather than others. In that sense, terminology is often a stake in these discursive games. Hence, we argue that several of these concepts have poor analytical value and are of little help in understanding the situation in post-Euromaidan Ukraine. We use the discussion on these concepts as a springboard to develop our own analytical model, based on communications and media theory and focusing on actors, media forms, and stories. This gives us a unique position to discuss the management of meaning and information from particular empirical entry points.

In chapter 2 we direct our attention to the *actors*, those who are "telling all the stories," to quote the legendary Hungarian American mass communications scholar George Gerbner (2010). According to Gerbner, we are cultivated into society, formed by the mass of stories that are told. Therefore, it is important to know who the storytellers are, what their motivations are, and within what frameworks they formulate their narratives. We discuss some of the agents involved in information management on the Ukrainian side, narrating material in English for international audiences. We propose that Russia's aggression has engaged an entirely new set of actors in the management of information, coming from the PR business, journalism, corporate finance, and, most notably, the voluntary sector. These new actors bring professional ideas and work routines from their fields of origin, which impact the practice and expressive character of what has been termed information warfare.

In chapter 3 we turn to the *forms* of information management and discuss how information is created in niche media before it takes form in mass media stories. We look at those communications platforms employed by the agents accounted for in chapter 2—that is, the media technologies and forms that precede the images and stories that are eventually relayed to international audiences. In a highly mediatized world, the mass media are also mediatized, meaning that there is a high degree of what Jay Bolter and Richard Grusin (2000) call "remediation," where images circulate from niche media to mass media. This remediation of images means that the narratives are formed in contexts and circumstances under which the niche media operate before they meet a larger mass audience. In this chapter we follow some of these processes of remediation and discuss the implications for the narratives that eventually reach the mainstream media of broadcast television and the press (in both print and online forms). This involves social media such as Facebook, Twitter, and VKontakte, as well as streamed television services that deliver footage for international news broadcasters, which reframe the images for the commercial and international framework in which they operate. It also includes presentational media such as PowerPoint, where discourses and images are formed and tested before being distributed more widely in advertising and mass media.

In chapter 4 we look at the actual *stories* and contents produced by the agents presented in chapter 2, with the help of the media forms discussed in chapter 3. We discuss the contents and information related to several particular events taking place between 2014 and 2017. Quite unexpectedly, many of these communicative efforts led up to and converged around an event that usually occurs outside the context of political controversy: the Eurovision Song Contest, held in Kyiv in May 2017. The international media attention surrounding this event was exploited by activist groups as well as by state authorities in both Russia and Ukraine. Our analysis builds on interviews with mass media representatives, PR consultants, political administrators, and brand designers but also on branding material, including the design of logotypes. In terms of policy, the events and communicative actions described are attempts to control narratives about Ukraine, and we discuss the nature and character of the actions as well as which domestic and foreign audiences the narratives were aimed at.

Chapter 5 summarizes our analysis of actors, media forms, and stories. Here, we widen the scope to discuss the fact that in a highly globalized world, information management and policy take new forms, involve new agents, and are managed on new types of communication platforms. This means that the power and control of information are increasingly diffused. The rise of large-scale media platform companies undermines the monopolies that nation-states once had on the control of information; access to media production technologies by civil society organizations makes it easier for them to bypass gatekeepers such as traditional news media outlets; and the flow of people between corporations and governmental departments introduces new practices and communication strategies. We conclude the chapter and the book with a discussion of how our study contributes to an understanding of the contemporary informational state and its specific characteristics.

NOTES ON METHOD

This book is based on more than six years of field research on branding, propaganda, and information and meaning management in Ukraine, from 2013 through 2019. Contextually, it also builds on our previous research on branding and soft power in India and Estonia. This may appear to be a rather simple and straightforward background, but describing the methodology, methods, and research material of this study is a delicate matter.

Sociologist Robert Merton once described a fairly common experience in qualitative research. Sometimes during the research process, by chance or coincidence, something unanticipated, surprising, or anomalous happens that changes the original context of the project and sends the researcher in a new direction of inquiry. It piques the researcher's curiosity, leads him or her along unplanned paths, and provokes new insights. Merton called this unanticipated but important component of research the "serendipity pattern" (1948, 506–509). What Merton had in mind was primarily the effect of such empirical findings on sociological theory. During later decades, the concept has occasionally been recycled among anthropologists, usually as a strategy for taking advantage of unexpected happenings and following coincidental encounters or new paths that might occur during ethnographic fieldwork (Hardtmann 2009; Hazan and Hertzog 2011; Rivoal and Salazar 2013). Some would even claim that serendipity constitutes "the essence of field-work research" (Pieke 2000, 138).

The serendipitous moment in the early phase of our research is rather obvious. The dramatic and unexpected Euromaidan events took place less than a year into our research and offered a unique opportunity to study meaning management in turbulent times. It certainly changed the direction of our research radically. Furthermore, almost out of necessity, serendipity had to remain the most characterizing methodological approach for our continuing research in Ukraine. No one could anticipate what would evolve out of these tumultuous events. It was not possible to demarcate a stable research field, and there was no way to plan exactly where and when to observe, who to meet, and what material to study. We had to be open to whatever we encountered. The guiding principle during these years of field research was to follow up on things that aroused our curiosity. We often interviewed people, read documents, studied media contents, and made ethnographic observations in a rather improvised manner. Moreover, several accounts in this book come from experiences that took place on the way to a formal meeting in an office, a stroll around Kyiv on a Sunday afternoon, or even a visit to a restaurant after a long day of interviewing government officials. A list of "research materials" would be highly deceptive and would not be exhaustive. In the chapters that follow, we refer to these interviews and observations, but needless to say, although the material that appears in this book follows our aims and our arguments, it does not reflect the totality of our empirical data.

Over the course of our study of information and meaning management in Ukraine, we made some decisive research choices. Most importantly, we deliberately focused on communication initiatives directed toward an international English-speaking audience. Our interest in these issues derived from the Ukrainian branding efforts around Euro2012 and the broadcast ads on BBC and CNN. Our initial interest was in analyzing nation branding efforts, which are, by nature, directed to an international audience of tourists, investors, and political stakeholders. Focusing on internationally oriented communication was also a choice of necessity, as neither of us speaks Ukrainian or Russian. To overcome our linguistic shortcomings, we worked with postdocs and students who are native Ukrainian and Russian speakers, and they assisted us with translations and cultural explanations. However, the politicians, media executives, journalists, PR consultants, academics, activists, and others we interviewed were well educated and, with few exceptions, spoke very good English. Many of the formal interviews we conducted were thus "elite" interviews with people in the capacity of their occupations or functions (Radway 1989), as distinct from interviews with everyday media users or audiences. Analytically, we treated the interviews as both "source" and "discourse"; that is, our informants contributed factual information and explanation, but equally important was how they phrased or formulated this information and how they characterized, for example, brand design or information strategy and policy (see Bolin 2003).

Although we were often close to the communication activities and actors in Ukraine, we also observed the events from a distance. For the most part, we followed the drama in and about Ukraine from Stockholm. This is, after all, a study of communication initiatives that are public and available through the internet or social media, and we followed the flow of news through regular channels as well as more specialized sources. Our frequent visits to Ukraine were usually instigated by something we learned about from a distance that prompted us to travel to Kyiv—only a two-hour flight from Stockholm—and get a closer look. Thus, during a period of six years, we traveled to Ukraine at least two or three times a year and met people involved in several organizations and particular communication activities. Initially, these meetings took the form of formal interviews, but after meeting repeatedly with the same people, the interactions became more casual.

Of course, our approach is also marked by our training in anthropology (Per Ståhlberg) and film and media studies (Göran Bolin), and most of our previous research has been qualitative and ethnographically inspired. Rather than being driven by theory-informed hypotheses, we were inspired by our own curiosity about branding and information and meaning management and the people involved in such activities. We see these practices as being played out in a complex field of social relations in the context of political tensions, international relations, and economic dynamics. This is also how we account for them in the chapters that follow, starting with the broader theoretical framework and approach in chapter 1.

CONTENTIOUS CONCEPTS

Despite its short history as an independent country, Ukraine experienced several tumultuous political events even before the full-scale invasion by Russia in February 2022. Three of these are linked to protests initiated on Maidan Nezalezhnosti (Independence Square) in Kyiv, and in popular discourse they are often called revolutions. The first of these, the Revolution on Granite, was a student protest that occurred in October 1990, the year before Ukraine became an independent nation-state following the Soviet Union's collapse in 1991. The name referred to the students' raising of tents on the granite steps leading to the square's Lenin monument. The peaceful protest resulted in the government's acceptance of the protesters' demands. This was followed shortly by the breakup of the Soviet Union and Ukraine's independence as a sovereign nation-state (Yekechyk 2015, 1–2). A national referendum took place 1 December 1991, and an overwhelming majority supported the Act of Declaration of Independence—of the 82 percent of the electorate that participated, more than 90 percent voted in favor of the act (Magocsi 2010, 724ff.). While it remained careful in its relations with Russia, the government of Leonid Kuchma took a few steps toward building a Ukrainian national identity, such as issuing decrees of "decommunization" of the Soviet past (Oliinyk and Kuzio 2021, 808).

The Orange Revolution, named for the campaign color of the political opposition, started with large protests in 2004 against a rigged election and, more generally, against corruption in the government. The discovery that Viktor Yanukovych had manipulated election results in his favor in November 2004 led to massive protests. These protests were successful, and a new and fair election was held, resulting in victory for the opposition candidate, Viktor Yuschenko, and his prime minister, Yulia Tymoshenko. The Yuschenko government went further in distancing Ukraine from Russia and building a Ukrainian national history. A particular focus was Holodomor, the Great Famine of 1932–1933, caused by Joseph Stalin's decision to curb the farmers' resistance to his agricultural policy (Apple-baum 2017; Reid 1997). A Holodomor museum was built, and the Insti-tute of National Remembrance was launched (Kasianov 2022; Oliinyk and Kuzio 2021, 808).

However, Yuschenko became increasingly unpopular, and in 2010 he lost the election to his predecessor and former rival, Yanukovych, who regained power. Yanukovych's main opponent, Yulia Tymoshenko, had received almost as many votes as he did, and the following year Tymoshenko was arrested and jailed. This jailing of an opposition politician overshadowed much of the discourse about Ukraine for the years 2011–2013 and contributed to the country's image as corrupt, undemocratic, and unable to move forward (see Ståhlberg and Bolin 2016).

The third so-called revolution occurred when, contrary to expectations, President Yanukovych did not sign the association agreement with the European Union in November 2013. He was subsequently ousted and fled to Russia. In Ukraine these violent events are called the Revolution of Dig-nity, but in the rest of the world they are more commonly known as the Euromaidan Revolution.

Revolution is, of course, a very strong word for conceptualizing a political event. Although it had a prominent place in early twentieth-century politi-cal discourse, the term *revolution* was used rather sparsely in national histo-ries, reserved only for radically restructuring events that entirely transformed societies and were loaded with visualizations, myths, and iconography. Revo-lution is thus about *parametric* changes on a systemic level, where the constitu-tive parts of the system are reorganized. Changes within the framework of an existing system can thus be described as *nonparametric*, where some features of a system (e.g., a state) are reformed but the system itself remains intact (Braman 2006, 260ff.). The most famous revolutions of the parametric kind are no doubt the French Revolution of 1789 and the Russian Revolution of 1917. However, many nation-states around the world historicize their birth in terms of revolutions (e.g., the American Revolution of 1776). It may be significant that Ukraine has been described as having had three revolutions in the last three decades. So how are we to understand these events today, and what significance do they have domestically as well as internationally?

The Orange Revolution may be the most internationally well known of these three events, and perhaps it should first be understood in a global context rather than in relation to other Ukrainian events. For some years around the turn of the millennium, revolutions named after colors and flowers occurred in many places, not least in the former Soviet states. Thus, the Orange Revolution is often remembered together with the Rose Revolution in Georgia and the Tulip Revolution in Kyrgyzstan, perhaps recalling the earlier Velvet Revolution in Czechoslovakia and the even earlier Carnation Revolution in Portugal or related to the later Jasmine Revolution in Tunisia. These names might have divergent backgrounds, but they were enthusiastically adopted and popularized by the international media, and they are often markers for domestic celebrations. Their names suggest that these were good revolutions, usually described as peaceful and nonviolent protests against totalitarian regimes.[1] This attention from the global mass media has framed these upheavals within a common narrative structure that not only represents the events but also affects the events themselves.

These colorful political events also contributed to a reinterpretation of the concept of revolution, which, to say the least, had not been unanimously embraced in the capitalist world. In a sense, the concept was appropriated by liberal ideology and used in discursive combat with regimes in countries with histories of anticapitalist revolutions. Thus, the leadership in Russia was not fond of the color revolutions, especially those taking place in the immediate vicinity of Russia, such as the Orange Revolution in Ukraine (Finkel and Brudny 2012b). In this case, however, it was not merely a struggle over words. The Orange Revolution in 2004 was directed against a Russia-backed regime that was replaced with a more Western-friendly one.

At the time of the Euromaidan upheaval, it was not far-fetched to relate it to the Orange Revolution of a decade earlier. First, the political issue was almost the same: popular discontent with a corrupt regime backed by Russia. Second, several of the same political actors reappeared in this drama: Yanukovych, the politician accused of fraud during the Orange Revolution, was back in power as president, and many of the individuals now demanding his resignation had been active in the previous revolt. Third, although it happened within a less optimistic conjuncture of global processes, it made sense to symbolically link the Euromaidan Revolution with an era that had positive connotations in world politics. Relabeling it the Revolution of Dignity and associating it with both the colorful revolts (Orange Revolution) and protests against the Soviet regime (Revolution on Granite) emphasized that this was a legitimate uprising against an unjust regime, but with a sharp edge toward Russia.

For a while at least, the events occurring at Maidan Nezalezhnosti in Kyiv in 2013–2014 resembled revolutionary scenarios from earlier times: dramatic TV footage and press photos communicated to international audiences, showing barricades, burning piles of tires, violence, blood, and death. As if the images did not speak for themselves, foreign correspondent Elin Jönsson, reporting from Kyiv for Swedish television, anchored their meaning by exclaiming, "It looks like a revolution" (Sveriges Television 2013).

The visual comparison to the revolt of a decade earlier was striking. Images from the Orange Revolution showed peaceful demonstrations in sunny daylight. Protesters were smiling, and the color orange was everywhere—on flags, banners, scarves, caps, and balloons. Ten years later, the images were dark, often shot at night. They showed angry or threatened protesters fighting with the police, surrounded by clouds of black smoke. Now the flags and banners were blue and yellow (the colors of Ukraine's national flag) and black and red (in this context, symbolizing right-wing nationalism, not anarchism), and of course, there was the flag of the European Union with its twelve yellow stars against a clear blue background.

Several months later, when the revolt was over and the regime had changed, remnants of the violent clashes between the protesters and the police were still left on the Maidan and neighboring roads. We returned to Kyiv in June 2014 and strolled among the burnt-out vehicles and debris from the barricades. Military tents had been raised, and remaining revolutionaries in tattered uniforms were watching over the space (figure 1.1). Along the streets, entrepreneurial citizens were trading revolution-inspired merchandise, including toilet paper and doormats printed with the faces of Vladimir Putin and Yanukovych. The site looked like an open-air theme park of a violent revolution—although memorials with pictures of fallen heroes reminded visitors that this had been real. Later, the people killed during the fights were honored as the "Heavenly Hundred."

Importantly, the impression of the Euromaidan Revolution as dark and violent is not the complete picture. Instead, it may be an image that, with time, has become a mediated memory. As several scholars have concluded, the events that took place in central Kyiv were very fragmented; just a few streets away from the battle, peaceful activities occurred simultaneously. Furthermore, the three months of protests passed through several phases with different atmospheres (Stepnisky 2020). Thus, the dark and violent images belong largely to the second phase, from mid-January to mid-February.

Figure 1.1
Maidan Nezalezhnosti, 2 June 2014.
Photo by authors.

Before that, the Maidan protests seemed rather peaceful. At the outset, Maidan had all the trappings of a peaceful occupation. It drew on familiar repertoires from the peaceful Orange Revolution and other nonviolent protests: tents, political speeches, marchers with flags and decorated posters, musical performances, humorous and satirical graffiti, and nonviolent defiance of the police (Stepnisky 2020, 86).

But the question of how to conceptualize the three Ukrainian upheavals remains. In media and communication studies of the early twentieth century, revolutions (as well as world wars) have often been understood from the perspective of information management and related, in particular, to the concept of propaganda. Revolutionaries such as Lenin, Stalin, and Mao have been regarded as skillful communicators of their eras, and revolutionary posters, artworks, slogans, and films have become standard examples of propaganda aesthetics and rhetoric (Kenez 1985). Just like the word *revolution*, *propaganda* became a key term characterizing the world's predicament during much of the twentieth century. "This is the age of propaganda" is the opening phrase in a classic study of protests in the US during the Great Depression, and its title combines the two key concepts: *World Revolutionary Propaganda: A Chicago Study* (Lasswell and Blumenstock 1939).

In this respect, something changed with the new millennium or perhaps earlier, with the end of the Cold War. As Colin Sparks (1998) notes in his account of changes occurring after the fall of the Berlin Wall in 1989, revolution had become a metaphor applied to dramatic developments in several domains, such as the information revolution, and its adjective form was used in marketing campaigns. Sparks helpfully distinguishes four ways to regard the revolutionary events taking place in eastern Europe around 1989: "total transformation," indicating social as well as political change; "social (counter)revolution," indicating social but not political change; "political revolution," indicating political but not social change; and "what revolution?" indicating neither political nor social change (1998, 78ff.). After a thorough analysis of the mass media and their organizational structures and staffing, the legal system surrounding the mass media, and the role of civil society at the time, Sparks concludes that, at least in the four Visegrad countries (Poland, Hungary, Czech Republic, and Slovakia) at the center of his analysis, there is strong support for the political revolution perspective; that is, despite the changes made in the political and economic systems, the "oppressive and exploitative social relations that were characteristic of the older order" were not fundamentally altered. The mass media constitute a case in point: organizationally, they changed from state television and a state-controlled press into public service broadcasting companies and a liberal press, but they were run by the same *nomenklatura* as during communist times (Sparks 1998, 188).

Propaganda as a concept occurs several times in Sparks's account, but it is referred to only in relation to the communist pasts of the analyzed countries. The same is true of the color revolutions around the world, which are rarely analyzed from the perspective of propaganda—and when they are, it is always the threatened authoritarian regime that is propagandist, not the revolutionaries. This was the situation in Ukraine during and after the Euromaidan Revolution: communication from the new regime would not be termed propaganda, but communication from its critics would be. Thus, the two key concepts from the twentieth century remain in the vocabulary of the twenty-first century, but they have shifted location and, perhaps, meaning. Furthermore, they are hardly the dominant concepts for characterizing the present. Many other words are competing for that status. Instead of a *revolution* in Ukraine some might discuss this in terms of *conflict* or *crisis*; the terms *disinformation, fake news,* and *information war* are competing with the concept of *propaganda.*

WORDS, WORDS, WORDS . . .

The words *revolution* and *propaganda* have thus been unstable, controversial, and challenged terms for a long time. Propaganda has been studied since the early days of mass communication research (Lippmann [1922] 1946; Lasswell [1927] 1971; Bernays [1928] 2005). In their remarkably nuanced treatise of world revolutionary propaganda in the 1930s, Harold Lasswell and Dorothy Blumenstock explain that there is only a slight difference between propaganda and what is usually regarded as its antonym: "Propaganda is the manipulation of symbols to control controversial attitudes; education is the manipulation of symbols (and of other means) to transmit accepted attitudes (and skills)" (1939, 10). Their point is that what is propaganda in one context is education in another. For example, the advocacy of communism is propaganda in America but education in the Soviet Union, while the propagation of individualism is propaganda in the Soviet Union but education in America.

Several decades later, at the height of the Cold War, Jacques Ellul reflected on another challenge related to the phenomenon of propaganda. On the one hand, "propaganda is usually regarded as an evil [but to] study anything properly one must put aside ethical judgements"; on the other hand, propaganda becomes a completely useless concept if it includes any effort to communicate ideas with the intention of influencing people's attitudes, because then "everything is propaganda" (Ellul 1965, x–xi). This insight from the twentieth century is useful when studying policy and meaning management in the present; the fight over words has hardly decreased.

But why do people fight over words? Why is it important to quarrel over whether something should be called propaganda or education? The reason is that words have power. Words have the performative power to do things, as John Austin ([1955] 1975) famously theorized. In a general sense, then, words are the tools of symbolic power, as elaborated by Pierre Bourdieu (1991) in his *Language and Symbolic Power.* They are the stakes in the game, and the discursive battles and negotiations are the objects of analysis. The battle over words is a battle over who can define situations, who can describe the order of a specific society. The power to define situations is no small matter. How people frame their social interaction by way of a common definition of the situation has profound consequences for how they act in society, as famously captured in the Thomas theorem: "If men define situations as real, they are real in their consequences" (Thomas and Thomas 1928; cf. Merton 1995).[2]

The powers discussed by Austin, Bourdieu, and William and Dorothy Thomas could all fit under the umbrella of symbolic power. Sandra Braman calls this the type of power that shapes human behavior "by manipulating the material, social, and symbolic worlds via ideas, words, and images." However, Braman adds a more profound dimension of power—namely, "informational power," which she defines as the ability to manipulate other forms of power (i.e., instrumental, structural, and symbolic power) and thus effect paradigmatic change on a systems level (2006, 25ff.). Our analysis takes place largely on the level of symbolic power, but we return to the question of informational power in the final chapter.

The analyst of culture and society should be sensitive to the words he or she uses for analysis and should avoid falling into the discursive trap of using the jargon of the object of analysis. Revolution, propaganda, nation branding, and soft power are all concepts used in games of power to describe things and relations in certain terms rather than others. They can be used to elevate one's own position, gain advantages, and privilege one's place on the field of competition. Conversely, they can be used to undermine the position of one's adversaries. For the analyst, this has profound consequences, and like Bourdieu, one should seek at all costs to avoid the "received ideas and spontaneous sociology" that restrict the analysis and cause it to be performed in the language of the object of analysis itself ([2012] 2020, 3). Bourdieu makes this point several times in his work and in interviews (see, e.g., Bourdieu 1990), and he holds that the social sciences (especially sociology) present a special difficulty because many of the concepts are used in everyday parlance. One could argue that this is an even bigger problem in the field of media and communication: everybody has experiences with media, so everybody has opinions about how the media work and how they should be valued. The high degree of connectivity between analytical approaches and media practices means that practical concepts from the field of media enter into analytical language. Many of the concepts examined in this book are of that nature.

The meanings of words, however, are not stable over time. Fighting over words can lead to change, as words acquire new meanings or meanings change due to public use. This is evident in the *Oxford English Dictionary*, where one can read about the etymological history of words, when they first appeared in the English language, and when their meanings were altered. Raymond Williams, for example, famously devoted a whole book to following the trajectory of the word *culture* over nearly two hundred years, tracing its meanings among eighteenth-century writers and politicians such as Edmund Burke, nineteenth-century philosophers such as Jeremy Bentham or critics such as Matthew Arnold, and twentieth-century novelists and poets such as D. H. Lawrence, T. S. Eliot, and George Orwell. The introduction to this important text is worth quoting at length:

> In the last decade of the eighteenth century, and in the first half of the nineteenth century, a number of words, which are now of capital importance, came for the first time into common use, or, where they had already been generally used in the language, acquired new meanings. There is in fact a general pattern of change in these words, and this can be used as a special kind of map by which it is possible to look again at those wider changes in life and thought to which changes in language evidently refer. (Williams [1958] 1963, 13)

The words Williams has in mind are those whose meaning changed due to industrialization: *industry*, *democracy*, *class*, *art*, and *culture*. His point is that words change with society and are, in fact, a part of society. Words reflect how citizens think about society and how they think of themselves as part of society.

In line with Williams's analysis, a brief examination of the trajectory of *propaganda* as a concept is worthwhile. *Propaganda* was not always a negative word, and especially not in the part of the world where Ukraine is located. The word itself can be traced back to Cicero in the first century BC (Cull 2019, 172n17). As a systematic way of disseminating ideas, it was developed in 1539 by Ignatius of Loyola, founder of the Jesuit order, for "the defence and propagation of the faith" (quoted in Cull 2019, 9), thus bringing the concept of *propaganda fide* into the language of the church. It was gradually institutionalized "to coordinate missionary activity" (10), and in 1622 Pope Gregory XV founded the *Congregatio de propaganda fide*, consisting of a committee of cardinals responsible for foreign missions—that is, a committee for the propagation of the true faith. However, with the rise of mass media and fears related to mass society, *propaganda* acquired less positive connotations, and since then, its dominant meaning has been negative (Jowett and O'Donnell 1992, 82ff.).

In addition to words having different meanings at different points in time, there are regional variations to consider. In the revolutionary Soviet Union, for example, the word *propaganda* had positive connotations, and propaganda was used systematically to spread the socialist ideology to remote parts of the country. Propaganda as a concept was most often accompanied by the concept of agitation, and in the writings of Lenin and others, the two words were often used synonymously. However, Marxist thinker Georgi Plekhanov sought to distinguish them:

> Agitation is also propaganda, but propaganda that takes place in particular circumstances, that is in circumstances in which even those who would not normally pay any attention are forced to listen to the propagandist's words. Propaganda is agitation that is conducted in the normal everyday course of the life of a particular country. Agitation is propaganda occasioned by events that are not entirely ordinary and that provoke a certain upsurge in the public mood. ([1891] 1983, 103)

Plekhanov's distinction seems to be based on propaganda being active in the "formation of people's minds" (to use the words of Ellul [1965]), whereas agitation supports the formation of people's actions. Propaganda, then, is the theory, while agitation is the goal-oriented practice (cf. Kremer and Martov [1896] 1983, 203).

The two concepts merged in the practice of agitprop—agitation propaganda. The main instrument for agitprop was the cinema, and montage was the specific technique adopted by young filmmakers. Film, Lenin had argued, was the most important of the arts, but raw film was scarce, so enthusiastic young filmmakers had to make use of whatever was available. Clips from old films, shot for a variety of purposes, were then used in recombination to achieve new meanings. When juxtaposed, these clips could be combined in ways that produced new meanings. The goal was to produce an effect that redirected the audience's mind in the desired direction. Filmmaker Sergei Eisenstein became the main theorist of the montage, having developed it in *Strike* (1924), *October* (1927), and the pathbreaking *Battleship Potemkin* (1925) (Furhammar and Isaksson 1968, 16ff.). The massacre on the stairs in Odesa (located in contemporary Ukraine) is probably one of the most famous scenes in film history and is significant for Eisenstein's montage style, which he later theorized in his collection of essays *Film Form* ([1949] 1977).

Agitprop was thus a technology used to "provoke a certain upsurge," as Plekhanov phrased it, and spread the revolution around Russia's vast territory. Agitprop trains toured the countryside showing films to the (sometimes illiterate) masses. This was one art form in which famous directors such as Dziga Vertov and Aleksandr Medvedkin were deeply engaged (Heftberger 2015). However, agitprop also took the form of theater and poetry and was not confined to Soviet Russia; it was present in other parts of Europe, such as Weimar Germany. Many small theater companies assembled under the Arbeiter-Theater-Bund Deutschlands, which was affiliated with the Communist Party. The link to film was always close, however, and authors such as Bertolt Brecht transgressed the border between the two art forms.[3] It could be said that the art form itself, with its montage techniques and specific forms of agitation, paved the way for more recent forms of discursive strategical action and laid the foundation of Russian communicative practice. This art form is addressed in more detail in later chapters, but for now, it is enough to say that education and propaganda also have their cultural anchors and textual traditions.

US political scientist Harold Lasswell defined propaganda as "the management of collective attitudes by the manipulation of significant symbols" in his analysis of propaganda during World War I (1927, 627). More drastically, and perhaps because he was focusing on wartime propaganda, he thought of this as "the war of ideas on ideas" (Lasswell [1927] 1971, 12). His analysis is broad and includes various tropes and media forms in wartime propaganda, ranging from broadcasts to literature. And although there are examples of propaganda dating back to the Reformation and the invention of the printing press, with the industrialized warfare of World War I, propaganda became more important both internally, directed toward the domestic audience, and externally, directed toward the enemy. Governments needed to encourage military recruitment, ensure political support for the war among the citizenry, and mobilize public opinion to accept the moral righteousness of warfare (Vuorinen 2012). Conversely, propaganda was targeted toward the enemy with the aim to demoralize, destabilize public support, and sow seeds of doubt among the enemy's population. However, the foreign audience is not necessarily confined to the conflict region, such as when one party in a conflict feels the need to raise support or influence international public opinion (Schleifer 2012).

So, in the thinking of Lasswell and others, the phenomenon of propaganda deals with the intentional manipulation of meaning to direct attention, stir emotion, and produce hatred, adoration, or loyalty. As we have seen, however, the concept of propaganda is both descriptive and *constative,* in Austin's ([1955] 1975) meaning: a word used to establish something factual. But it also has performative power; it does something. For example, it blames the propagandist for twisting reality, for manipulating people into perceiving situations one way rather than another. As such, the word *propaganda* is part of propaganda practice.

Propaganda is thus mostly thought of as a descriptive word, but it is also involved in how social and political realities are presented. The same can be said of the word *revolution.* In his famous book *Keywords,* Williams observes an extension of its meaning and to what it is applied:

> Revolution and revolutionary and revolutionize have of course also come to be used, outside political contexts, to indicate fundamental changes, or fundamentally new developments, in a very wide range of activities. It can seem curious to read of "a revolution in shopping habits" or of the "revolution in transport," and of course there are cases when this is simply the language of publicity, to describe some "dynamic" new product. (1976, 273–274)

One could say that words are sometimes appropriated and recontextualized, not least into commercial contexts. As Williams notes, this had already happened with *revolution* in the early 1970s. Several decades later, when we encounter the word in a political context again, we should bear in mind that revolutions have passed through the world of commerce and acquired new connotations (while losing some older ones). The Revolution of Granite, the Orange Revolution, and the Revolution of Dignity are not simply the names of three moments in Ukraine's contemporary politics. These Ukrainian upheavals are labeled and interconnected with the subtlety of promotional skills familiar from the commercial world of advertising, branding, and public relations (PR). The names no longer connote only violence or tumult; they also have significations of attraction, youthfulness, and desire. It appears as if the revolution has been branded.

Two years after the Euromaidan revolt, the debris on Independence Square in Kyiv had long since been cleared. Although the country was still subjected to violent pressure from its powerful neighbor in the east, everyday life in the city seemed surprisingly normalized, though interspersed with details reminiscent of the tumultuous events. Permanent memorials to the "Heavenly Hundred" who died during the upheaval stood where the battles had been most intense, and government billboards along the main streets called attention to the ongoing war. In the busy underground shopping mall below the now famous square, an upscale restaurant had opened. The theme of the restaurant, called Ostannya Barykada (Last Barricade), was "three revolutions." Showcased on the walls were photos, news clippings, and various objects related to the three Ukrainian revolutions, including a printout of the Facebook posting that allegedly instigated the latest revolution (figure 1.2).

The restaurant took pride in serving 100 percent Ukrainian food and drinks, but the menu, handed to us by a waitress in traditional Ukrainian folk dress, also contained a proclamation. With sophistication, the text intertwined this commercial eatery with a story of majestic politics. It is worth citing the proclamation in full (including grammatical errors):

> The today's Ostannya Barikada is an art and gastronomic space, a place for free thinking people and representatives of the new generation which were born by three modern Ukrainian revolutions: Student Revolution on Granite in 1990, Orange Revolution in 2004 and the Revolution of Dignity in 2014.
>
> Ostannya Barykada is a platform for creating social and art projects, brainstorming, as well as for the inventing and implementing of the essential ideas.

Figure 1.2
Mustafa Nayem's Facebook posting, which allegedly instigated the last revolution, photocopied at the restaurant Ostannya Barykada, 18 October 2016.
Photo by authors

This is our fortress, a frontline where society is able to discuss long-term strategies of the country policy and work on the mistakes.

All three Ukrainian Maidan Revolutions showed the people's fascinating self-organization. We want to preserve that spirit of sympathy, altruism, social alertness and uprising which helped to create Ukrainian Revolutions of the last three decades.

The famous French philosopher Bernard-Henri Levy once said from the Maidan stage of 2014: "the heart of Europe beats in Kyiv." Only we being united can flush back the meaning and sense to such European values as freedom, democracy and tolerance.

On our bill is Taras Shevchencho's poem Zapovit and the slogan of all revolutions itself:

BORITESYA—POBORETE [STRUGGLE—YOU
SHALL OVERCOME]

The name Ostannya Barykada also carries connotations of an artistic movement with the same name, founded in the early 2000s, that has promoted Ukrainian culture, organized festivals and art exhibitions, and even produced a TV show. It also released a series of four CDs with songs by Ukrainian bands and musicians. The fourth—*Music Hundred*—was dedicated to the Euromaidan events. Notably, the movement's chairman, Oles Doniy, was one of the active organizers of the Revolution on Granite.

We return to this form of meaning-making later in this chapter, but to understand the changed semiotic meaning of revolution and the labeling of the upheavals in Ukraine, we need to expand the discussion and examine some other central concepts related to information policy in the contemporary world.

THE POWER OF REPRESENTATION

As we have shown, the concept of propaganda has been largely abandoned, mainly due to the negative connotations related to deceptive and false information and the manipulation of audiences. Few countries in the world now aspire to be "propaganda states."[4] Still, in a global world of alliances and trade agreements, governments want the rest of the world to have a favorable image of their countries, and they develop information policies to produce this image. Arguably, late modern globalization has fueled the need to navigate in relation to the countries with which one trades or wants to trade and the countries one might want to have as allies. Thus, during the last decades of the twentieth century, governments of nation-states started to worry about their reputation. These worries did not come from nowhere; they originated from lobbying activities within the fields of marketing and PR. Other concepts related to a government's promotion of a certain image of its nation-state have come into vogue, replacing propaganda.

In the second half of the twentieth century, *public diplomacy* was launched as an alternative, less negatively burdened concept to describe a practice that had in fact been around since World War II, carried out, for example, by the United States Information Agency (USIA). Public diplomacy should thus be understood as a "democratic equivalent to the word 'propaganda'" (Cull 2019, 12) or, in the words of James Pamment, as "diplomatic advertising" (2013, 2). Public diplomacy is generally presented as an attractive activity and is often juxtaposed to propaganda; indeed, Edmund Guillon, the US diplomat who coined the term, would "have liked to call it 'propaganda,'" but he realized the word's negative connotations made that difficult (Cull 2019, 12). Consequently, public diplomacy is often described as "based on truth," whereas "propaganda selects truth"; public diplomacy is "often two-way" and "tends to be respectful," whereas "propaganda is seldom two-way" and "assumes that others are ignorant or wrong" (Cull 2019, 13). Public diplomacy research is a scholarly field that has grown out of diplomatic practice (Pike 2021, 7) and therefore often has an administrative slant (Lazarsfeld 1941), in the sense that it asks questions posed from within the practice itself, often with the aim of refining techniques or contributing to the development of diplomatic practice. However, the administrative-critical dimension is seldom either-or; rather, it consists of points along a continuum. The degree to which scholars are either responding to practical problems within public diplomacy (e.g., Entman 2008; Melissen 2005) or taking a more analytically critical stand (e.g., Pamment 2013; Surowiec 2016) is an open empirical question.

If public diplomacy is an activity and a practice, the resource it manages is *soft power*, a concept developed by political scientist Joseph Nye (2004) to define a country's ability to affect others with attraction and persuasion. In the United States, soft power rests on the soft resources of American culture, values, and morals. Despite its undertone of cultural imperialism, soft power is usually understood as a sympathetic, even pleasant form of power, and state authorities around the world have happily appropriated the concept (Hannerz 2016, 193–207). Nye himself expressed surprise when Chinese president Hu Jintao "told the Chinese Communist Party's 17th Party

Congress in 2007 that his country needed to increase its soft power" (Nye 2014, 20).[5] However, appropriation of an analytical concept into political practice blurs its meaning and reduces its analytical power to its descriptive dimensions, since all forms of its use will be interpreted within the framework of the political field of social action.

Nye (2008) followed up on his ideas about soft power by relating this specific type of power to the practice of public diplomacy. A country's soft power rests, according to Nye, on three pillars: its culture, its political values, and its foreign policies. The means by which a country can impact these three parameters is public diplomacy. Nye points to new communication technologies as contributing to the rise of public diplomacy. Initially, this meant radio that could broadcast to foreign audiences. Since then, the repertoire of available media has increased manifold, and social media in particular have become a means of acquiring international influence. Arguably, the presence of new media also changes the practices of soft power, producing hybrid forms that combine desire and fear (Surowiec 2017).

Public diplomacy and soft power rest on a political logic of power by attraction and the ability to dominate, or at least influence, other countries. It is a logic of international relations. The related phenomenon of *nation branding* can be described as a more campaign-oriented practice whereby governments, PR consultants, media organizations, and corporate businesses join forces to develop information policy through the promotion of a favorable image of a particular nation-state (Bolin and Ståhlberg 2010, 79). Nation branding as a concept and a phenomenon appeared in the early 1990s, advocated by entrepreneurial scholars at business schools in the UK and US who were also engaged in selling their consultancy services to governments (Aronczyk 2013). Consultant-scholars such as Wally Olins (2002), Keith Dinnie (2008), and Simon Anholt (2005, 2007) have, on the one hand, constructed assessment systems to measure the image value of nation-states on the international market and, on the other hand, used these systems to convince their customers—governments in different parts of the world—of the need to launch branding campaigns to put their specific countries "on the map."

Early examples of this specific practice include Brand Estonia, the campaign initiated by the Estonian government in 2001. At the time, Estonia had just won the Eurovision Song Contest (ESC), and according to tradition, it would host the event the following year. Estonia was the first post-Soviet country to win the hugely popular contest. Having regained its independence after the demise of the Soviet Union in 1991, the small country of 1.3 million inhabitants was trying to transform its economy through what President Mart Laar (1996) described as economic "shock therapy"—a combination of austerity and neoliberal economic policy. In this process, the ESC victory was extremely timely and offered a window of opportunity, as the rest of Europe would be focused on Estonia's capital, Tallinn, when the event was held there in May 2002.

The Brand Estonia campaign, executed by the British consultancy firm Interbrand, was one of the first nation branding campaigns. As such, it has received widespread attention from researchers and is probably the most covered campaign in the field of nation branding studies.[6] No doubt, this is also due to Estonia's policy, based on the Nordic model, of allowing public access to governmental documents. As a result, the campaign material, including the bilingual brand book *Eesti Stiil/Estonian Style*, was accessible online. Similar to the research on Estonia, most nation branding research is based on case studies of single campaigns or individual countries. Much attention has been paid to post-Soviet countries in eastern Europe, presumably because they share the historical conditions of being young nation-states with short histories of sovereignty and have sought to shake off their Soviet past and "rebrand" themselves as competitors in the global market for tourist and investor attention. This research includes the analyses by Volcic (2008) on post-Yugoslav countries, Aronczyk (2007) and Surowiec (2016) on Poland, Graan (2013) on Macedonia, Volcic (2012) and Volcic and Andrejevic (2011) on Slovenia, Kaneva and Popescu (2011) on Romania and Bulgaria, and Kaneva (2018) on Kosovo.

There are fewer works that seek to advance the theoretical understanding of nation branding. Furthermore, and as we discuss at length elsewhere (Bolin and Ståhlberg 2015), despite the fact that much branding research is conducted by media and communications scholars, the importance of mediation (as a communicative process) and the role of media (as technologies and organizations) is seldom theorized. The media are treated mainly as neutral platforms acted on by governments and brand professionals. This is a pity because the affordances carried by various media technologies, and the way they are organized, are vital to their ability to influence and stir up emotion and thus contribute to informational power, in Braman's (2006) sense.

To a large extent, soft power, public diplomacy, and nation branding involve commercial actors and institutions in communication efforts. The people involved are thus not trained in political communication to persuade citizens; rather, their backgrounds are in PR and advertising, practices aimed to promote desire among consumers. Through this influence, we witness the rise of the "brand state" (Van Ham 2001), and this conflation of the political and the commercial has been observed and theorized by several scholars. Pawel Surowiec (2016), for example, discusses this "new form of statecraft" within the framework of a "promotional culture" in his book *Nation Branding, Public Relations and Soft Power*. However, the idea that countries can be sold on a market and that their citizens can become props in this specific promotional culture met with criticism from cultural debaters and academics, especially those within what Nadia Kaneva (2011) calls the critical paradigm of nation branding studies. Within this paradigm, criticism of the practice of branding nations quickly developed, based on the argument that these activities commercialized and commodified national identities and produced a form of "commercial nationalism" (Volcic and Andrejevic 2011) or "national identity lite" (Kaneva and Popescu 2011). However, proponents of this type of information management quickly picked up on this criticism, and the concept of nation branding was largely abandoned within the practice field, paralleling the abandonment of propaganda (Jowett and O'Donnell 1992). Practitioners within the field launched alternative concepts such as competitive identity, brand management, or reputation management. Anholt (2007), who claims to have coined the concept of nation branding, soon abandoned it in favor of the concept of competitive identity.

Since public diplomacy research has its basis in practice, the main focus is often on the production side of the communication circuit, the "institutional practice and behaviour" (Pike 2021, 8), rather than on reception. In this, research on public diplomacy and nation branding shares characteristics with other practice-oriented research fields such as journalism and education, which focus on journalistic practice or didactic practical problems in the classroom. This is, of course, highly legitimate, but it means that some approaches are privileged before others. It also means that concepts are often picked up from practice jargon. They are thus descriptive, seeking to understand the nature of the activity—*what it is*—or policy oriented—how practice *should be*. In contrast, our interest lies in the implications of conceptual framing—*what concepts do*.

Braman argues that nation branding is a specific form of information policy, a part of the "continuing evolution of the informational state" (2019, 149). This is also true for the other communicative activities described above. Nation branding, public diplomacy, and the managing of soft power are all activities that concern strategic communication—that is, communication that is goal oriented and aimed at some form of influence or persuasion through images, stories, and the choice of terminology. Terminological choices thus have an impact on communication acts, and words can be either positively or negatively loaded.

SWEET OR TOXIC WORDS?

There is a paradoxical relation between older and newer concepts of information policy. In a sense, propaganda and public diplomacy are very similar concepts. Both rely on the idea that states exercise influence by disseminating meaning rather than by using hard, coercive power, whether military or economic. Indeed, several scholars regard propaganda and public diplomacy as interchangeable concepts (Soules 2015, 121). And Nye contextualizes soft power in almost exactly the same way Lasswell ([1927] 1971) characterized propaganda: as the third source of influence a state may use, the first two being military and economic power. Simultaneously, public diplomacy and propaganda are usually understood as different forms of communication because they are commonsensically loaded with contrasting normative assumptions. Propaganda is never pleasant, and today, few state leaders would describe their information strategies as propaganda: *we* seek to achieve soft power through public diplomacy; *they* produce propaganda—or worse, they manufacture fake information that we try to counter. In a sense, propaganda has more in common with coercive power than with soft power because it implies violating subjects' free will by imposing messages on them; in contrast, soft power supposedly works by "getting others to want the outcomes that you want" (Nye 2014, 20). While soft power and public diplomacy can be described as sweet, propaganda seems toxic.

Sweet and *toxic*: these two words capture the paradoxical impression of Ukrainian meaning management in the aftermath of the Euromaidan Revolution. Words, signs, and stories about Ukraine, transmitted to the rest of the world, have sometimes taken the form of uncontroversial images of pleasant people, resources, and places; this could be labeled soft power. At other times, communicated meanings have had an aggressive tone toward a perceived antagonist (usually Russia); in this case, they could be understood as forms of propaganda. However, these two types of communication have not always been handled as separate categories in different campaigns or by divergent actors. Furthermore, the character of meaning management seems rather fluid, consisting of ingredients that could be mixed in various proportions rather than belonging to discrete categories. At its extremes, this brew would taste sweet or toxic, but often it would fall somewhere in between. And occasionally, the same mixture could taste rather differently, depending on the palate of the consumer. Whatever the case, the chefs involved in meaning management seem to be concerned with several dimensions of affect—as much as effect.[7]

Concepts such as propaganda, nation branding, soft power, and public diplomacy—or, for that matter, fake news and information war—are limited as analytical tools. They are stakes in the game of attention and influence and are thus "contentious concepts" that deserve analytical consideration (Stade 2017). In this context, we consider them part of the study object, and through this measure we hope to achieve at least three things: First, we want to avoiding getting stuck in a rigid terminology loaded with normative assumptions and linked to rather obvious problems. Second, this intervention allows both greater sensibility toward the empirical material and the possibility of reconceptualizing the field of information management toward more strongly symbolic-oriented academic perspectives. Third, we want our analyses to include actions and practices of meaning management that occasionally seem nonsensical, playful, or unserious rather than thoroughly organized, strategically planned, and goal oriented. Particularly in chapter 4, we look at examples of content production with "affective dimensions" that would be difficult to grasp with concepts such as propaganda or public diplomacy (Kølvraa 2015).

In the following chapters, we look more closely at the fluidity of words and images and how the ambiguity of certain concepts is conditioning communicative policy and practice in the concrete conflictual situations Ukraine has experienced in the wake of Euromaidan. Importantly, words and concepts do not circulate as desultory units the communicator uses in a random manner. Words are symbolic components that may be used to build a signifying story. There is, of course, an academic concept for this level of sense-making: when words, events, people, and histories are linked to build a meaningful unity, they form a narrative. The term *narrative* has been popular in the social sciences for several decades, but much like *soft power*, it also circulates outside of the academy, especially in journalistic discourse. However, in Ukraine, it was at a university that we first came across the idea of conceptualizing the management of meaning in terms of conflictual narratives.

NARRATIVES AND THE MANAGEMENT OF MEANING

The National University of Kyiv-Mohyla Academy is one of Ukraine's more prestigious research universities, with a prehistory dating back to the early seventeenth century. After independence in 1991, it was reorganized in its present form, and it played a central role in both the Orange Revolution and the Euromaidan Revolution. Despite the university's relatively small size of around three thousand students, many of them have taken activist positions over the past couple of decades. Activism is especially intense in the Mohyla School of Journalism.

Yevhen Fedchenko is a professor of journalism and director of the Mohyla School of Journalism at the Kyiv-Mohyla Academy. He is also one of the initiators of StopFake—the fact-checking organization founded in March 2014 by students and faculty for the purpose of monitoring, countering, and debunking foreign—mainly Russian and Russian-supported—propaganda and fake news. StopFake is funded by individual donations and by grants from several international organizations, including the International Renaissance Foundation (part of George Soros's Open Society Foundation), National Endowment for Democracy (funded by the US Congress), Ministry of Foreign Affairs of the Czech Republic, Sigrid Rausing Trust, and UK embassy. StopFake is directed toward an international audience, and its fact-checking services were initially available in five languages: Ukrainian, Russian, Romanian, Spanish, and English. In 2021 this expanded to include Serbian, French, German, Dutch, Czech, Italian, Bulgarian, and Polish.

In November 2014 we visited the academy and the journalism department to learn more about the activities of StopFake and the role of faculty and students. Our conversation soon centered around the complexities of communication, the effect of news on opinions, the perils of journalists' angles, and the specific difficulties of debunking Russian news stories. Interestingly, Fedchenko talked about news stories as narratives. Russian narratives, he argued, are clever because they are seldom completely false; rather, they are twisted in a way that leads interpretations in certain directions. For example, when Russian media reported that the Ukrainian revolution was a fascist revolution and that the Ukrainian army was a fascist army, this was hard to debunk because there were admittedly battalions whose members were openly fascist. Most infamous in this respect was, at the time of our interview, the Azov battalion, a unit of Ukrainian volunteers that had also attracted far-right volunteers from all over the world. When the Russian media depicted the Ukrainian army as fascist, they were of course implying that these elements in the Azov battalion were representative of the whole army.[8]

Arguably, the narrative concept is a well-theorized part of textual analysis, developed from the interpretative approaches of comparative literature, film studies, structuralism, and Russian formalism. The way Fedchenko discusses it, however, is quite general and more in line with the conceptualization of narrative from political science and international relations literature, where the concept of *strategic narrative* has gained increased popularity in recent years.[9] Strategic narrative, as defined by the main proponents of the concept (and the ones most often referred to)—Alister Miskimmon, Ben O'Loughlin, and Laura Roselle (2013)—builds on theoretical and epistemological inspiration from Kenneth Burke's (1969) rhetoric. It consists of four components: character and actors, setting/environment/space, conflict or action, and resolution or suggested resolution. Following these components, the analysis of strategic narratives focuses on three levels: international systems narratives, which "describe how the world is structured, who the players are, and how it works," exemplified by "narratives such as the Cold War"; national narratives, which "set out what the story of the state or nation is, what values and goals it has," such as "the US as peace-loving"; and issue narratives, which "set out why a policy is needed and (normatively) desirable, and how it will be successfully implemented or accomplished" (Roselle, Miskimmon, and O'Loughlin 2014, 76).

Although the theory of strategic narratives contains some of the components of what could be called classic narrative theory, we find the concept of strategic narrative somewhat undertheorized. First, the lack of a temporal structure makes actors' relations incomprehensible or at least hard to explain. Relatedly, the absence of causal relations between events, contexts, and actions undermines its explanatory power. In our view, strategic narratives, as they are exemplified (e.g., the Cold War), are not narratives at all but perhaps discourses or apprehensions of the various positions of international actors (e.g., nation-states). Our analysis is thus based on a more classical tradition of narrative analysis. At its most basic, a narrative is a sequence of events assembled in a temporal flow to make a meaningful whole. Tzvetan Todorov (1969) famously defined a narrative as a sequence of interrelated events that unfolds from a state of equilibrium, with the introduction of a problem that is then solved and equilibrium is restored. Todorov, of course, was a literary critic, and his example was *Decameron*, but the "getting-in-and-out-of-trouble" principle of his narrative analysis has been proved to fit fictional film and television. Arguably, when we seek to understand the world around us, we try to make seemingly discrete events meaningful by relating them to one another, and many times this meaning construction takes the form of a coherent narrative, where the events we encounter have a causal relation. The logic of these constructions follows the narrative pattern of narratologists such as Todorov and Vladimir Propp ([1928] 1968), who famously deconstructed the Russian folktale into functional narrative elements and characters. A famous example of Proppian analysis of popular culture is Umberto Eco's examination of the novels of Ian Fleming, where he uses Proppian narrative analysis to reveal the novels' game-like structure in which James Bond "moves and mates in eight moves" (Eco 1981, 161). Another example is Janice Radway's ([1984] 1991) seminal critique of the romance novel, where she combines narrative and reception analysis.

Both Propp and Todorov have proved useful for the analysis of popular fiction, but they can also be used to analyze other genres, such as news. News reporting in both print and audiovisual media often employs tropes and characters that are functional in an overarching story and are made intelligible through familiar patterns of narration and generic conventions (Carey 1983; Schudson 1982, 2005; Dahlgren 1999). Narratives in the form of myths have been a main component of poststructural anthropology and semiotics, and they have also been used to analyze various types of live-broadcast media events. Daniel Dayan and Elihu Katz (1992) define *media events* as a unique television genre that disrupts the everyday routine with live broadcasts across all channels. These events are typically "organized outside of the media" and orchestrated by "public bodies with whom the media cooperate, such as governments, parliaments (congressional committees, for example), political parties (national conventions), [and] international bodies (the Olympic committee)"; they are "pre-planned" and "presented with reverence and ceremony" (Dayan and Katz 1992, 5–7). Media events, Dayan and Katz argue, are "ceremonial enactments of the bases of authority" in society, and their ritual function is one of reconciliation and reintegration (43).

This theory has been widely employed in media and cultural studies, and there are plenty of case studies on various kinds of media events, such as coronations, funerals, and popular culture events.

The theory of media events has been criticized for being, among other things, too functionalist. The most elaborate critique has been advanced in a series of articles by Nick Couldry (2000, 2003, 2006), who argues that, in addition to its functionalist bias, Dayan and Katz's work is affirmative and not critical enough of the media's power. Dayan and Katz do not deny that their theory is functionalist. This is indeed the main point of their analysis of societal integration. However, the claim that the theory therefore cannot deal with societal change is perhaps less true. In chapter 4 we highlight the development of this specific narrative theory and point to the subcategory of events that Dayan and Katz call "transformative."[10]

The media events theory has also been criticized for neglecting news events, and some have cited the 2001 terrorist attack on the Twin Towers in New York City as an example (Stepinska 2010). This criticism has also been at least partly acknowledged. Elihu Katz and Tamar Liebes discuss the "declining centrality of media events" in light of "three types of trauma that seemed to have resolutely moved to center-stage": terror, disaster, and war (2007, 159ff.). They also identify a fourth trauma that they deliberately set aside: revolution.

In its original conception, in the criticism, and in the theory's revision, the analysis of media events has emphasized the narrative unfolding of stories, following an inner dynamic. Because media events are preplanned, everybody understands what is about to happen (a coronation, a state funeral, the Olympic Games) and when it is going to happen, contributing to the "mass ceremony." The three types of events that Dayan and Katz label contests, conquests, and coronations have a narrative closing point: someone wins (and others lose), something is conquered (e.g., a peace deal between nation-states is closed), or someone is crowned. The general outcome of the event is thus known beforehand. In fact, it can be argued that the events themselves are orchestrated along narrative principles, ending with narrative closure.

This is also why Katz and Liebes's (2007) expansion of the media events theory fits uneasily into the original events theory. However, even if the outcome of a news event is less certain than, say, a funeral, this does not mean it is devoid of narrative elements. Most news stories have a fixed gallery of narrative functions in the Proppian sense. Most obviously there are heroes and villains—the good guys and the bad guys—but there are other functional characters as well, such as false heroes, donors, and helpers.

There are also clear narrative conventions related to news that have been analyzed within the framework of journalism studies. The "summary lead," for example, is a narrative convention that has developed over the years in print journalism (Schudson 1982). Similarly, the segmentation of broadcast news has been highlighted as a specific television format, but it also corresponds with non-news formats such as live entertainment television. John Ellis makes the important point that television narration is built on segments, which can be described as self-contained units with internal narrative structures that are assembled into larger wholes (programs). This is especially true in fictional TV series, but it also occurs in news broadcasts, where the news bulletin can be seen as "the first true use of the open-ended series format . . . endlessly updating events and never synthesising them" (Ellis 1992, 145). We have elsewhere extended this idea to live broadcasts of other genres such as election night coverage, game shows, and the Eurovision Song Contest (Bolin 2009). Likewise, foreign news is guided by "storylines," or overarching themes that help a correspondent select, contextualize, and present an event taking place in a designated region to make the reporting comprehensible to the audience (Hannerz 2004, 102ff.). Such narrative conventions are part of the various genre systems—the taken-for-granted "contract" between producers of stories and their audiences. They are thus important ingredients in the management of meaning; they direct audiences toward certain interpretations rather than others, but of course, they never determine how a story can be interpreted.

Within organizational communication one usually talks in terms of "information management," where the concept is a key tool in analyzing how corporations administer and control internal information flows to optimize activities (Choo 2006). Information management deals with "the control over how information is created, acquired, organised, stored, distributed, and used as a means of promoting, efficient and effective information access, processing, and use" (Detlor 2010, 103). The concept of information, however, implies the transmission of ideas from one sender to one or many receivers. When looking at communication practices in Ukraine, our approach is more interpretive and more in line with a ritual conception of communication. We emphasize meaning-making among those who construct messages. This is also why we emphasize the *management of meaning*. In this type of discursive management, concepts such as propaganda, persuasion, branding, disinformation, misinformation, fake news, and the like become stakes in a struggle for discursive dominance in informational space, rather than analytical tools.

To manage meaning, as we theorize it, indicates intentionality. However, as the following chapters show, intentionality varies among different agents, who might have similar yet slightly different motives for their communication efforts. These multiple motives and related meanings are then negotiated in the texts that result from these efforts, similar to how meaning is negotiated in reception. Meaning can never be determined among the receivers of messages, and what the sender has control over—whether that sender is an individual or an organization—is the composition of signs (although complex communication situations make total control difficult). As Sven Ross (2008) has argued with reference to Stuart Hall's (1973) encoding-decoding model, negotiations occur both at the moment of encoding and at the moment of decoding. What possible meaning is produced in the end is an empirical question. In the following chapters, we use the concept of management of meaning to highlight the intentionality and the will to use communicative tools strategically, while we reserve the concept of management of information to describe the activity by which individuals manage signs.

The management of meaning is an activity conducted by *agents* working with media technologies to construct narratives, discourses, and images. They do so within the framework of certain *forms of communication*. These constructions, and the forms they are based on, are managed at certain specific occasions—certain *events* that have to be understood in light of the contextual factors surrounding them. This is the analytical model we propose for the following chapters.

CONCLUSION

We opened this chapter by describing three tumultuous events that all started on the same square in Kyiv within three decades. It would, of course, be reasonable to ask why these events occurred, how they happened, or what their political and social consequences were. But instead, the perspective we have outlined is concerned mainly with understanding how the meanings of these events have been managed. Thus, we discussed how words are used—for example, by conceptualizing, linking, and labeling the three Ukrainian events as consecutive revolutions. In consonance with the discussion on narrativity in the last section, we should explain that line of reasoning.

When linked together, the three Ukrainian revolutions can be read as a story—a narrative moving from a beginning to an end and unfolding Ukraine's recent history in sequence. The story commences when the country is still part of an oppressive empire and times are hard and gray: the first revolution occurred "on granite." The second event took place during a period of expectations, when emancipating revolts were happening around the world; that revolution had the bright (but somewhat ambiguous) color of orange. The last event signified closure: the story came to an end, as that revolution meant the country had achieved dignity. The framing of these events as a narrative trope in which the Ukrainian nation-state gradually shakes off its Soviet legacy follows a narrative pattern similar to how film-maker Sergei Eisenstein illustrates the popular uprising in the famous Odesa steps scene of *The Battleship Potemkin* (1925). That scene ends in a montage of three statues of lions juxtaposed to rise from a resting to a standing position, illustrating the uprising against the oppressors. Similarly, one could interpret the narrativization of Ukraine's post-Soviet history in terms of the three revolutions.

Of course, the real story of Ukraine has no closure. At the time of this writing, a full-scale war is going on. Uncertainty reigns regarding Ukraine's political and economic future and even its sovereignty as a nation-state. Not least, the management of meaning about Ukraine is an activity conducted against a powerful aggressor with vast military and informational resources. In the following chapter we take a closer look at those who are formulating and telling the Ukrainian counternarrative.

THE MANAGERS OF MEANING

What is it that makes human beings human? My answer to that question is that human beings are the only creatures that we know (or I know) that live in a world erected by the stories we tell.
—George Gerbner (2010, 37)

In the wake of the Euromaidan Revolution, once the political situation had stabilized somewhat after Yanukovych's escape to Russia, the Ukrainian government under President Petro Poroshenko and Prime Minister Arseniy Yatsenyuk launched the Ministry of Information Policy (MIP) in December 2014. This was not an uncontroversial initiative, as can be imagined. Several journalists and media outlets, including the organization Reporters Without Borders, raised their voices against the formation of the Orwellian "Ministry of Truth" (Grytsenko 2014). Criticism was also raised by diplomats such as the US ambassador to Ukraine. The MIP remained active, however, until it was closed down in 2019 (although some of its functions were reactivated under the Ministry of Culture and Information Policy launched in 2020).

A Ministry of Information Policy is, of course, a state tool for formulating and communicating the state's policy, but in this case, it also had a reactive function "to combat biased information against Ukraine" (Interfax Ukraine 2014). During its active period, the MIP's communication strategy included embedding international journalists in the war zones in eastern Ukraine, restoring the communications infrastructure in the same area, nation branding campaigns, and the iArmy, a small unit with the task of managing the MIP's social media accounts. Formally, the MIP's responsibilities extended to the state-owned online television channel UATV, although it had a certain degree of editorial freedom, and the National News Agency of Ukraine—Ukrinform (ukrinform.net)—equipped with photo archives, a press center, and international correspondents. However, Ukrinform had a much longer history, having been founded in 1918 as the Bureau of Ukrainian Press.

The MIP was not the only state-related actor engaged in forming the official communication strategies of Ukraine. The Ministry of Culture, the Defense Ministry, and the Ministry of Foreign Affairs are also highly involved in shaping both the domestic and international images of Ukraine. Under these ministries are a number of institutes and projects, such as Ukraine Institute (ui.org.ua) and Ukraine Now (Ukraine.ua), devoted to shaping Ukraine's image and communicating it to international audiences.

Importantly, government authorities are not alone in this endeavor. Apart from the state-owned or state-controlled platforms, there are a number of nongovernmental organizations (NGOs), think tanks, and branding agencies involved in forming images and communicating information about Ukraine to international publics. Most famous is probably StopFake, the fact-checking and "fake news"–debunking organization created by faculty and students at the Mohyla School of Journalism, introduced in chapter 1. In addition, there are new online news providers such as Hromadske TV and Euromaidan Press, both of which were launched around the time of the Euromaidan Revolution. There is also the Ukraine Crisis Media Center (UCMC), a civic initiative introduced soon after the Euromaidan events; it started as a press center but has taken on a much broader role in meaning management.

All these organizations and initiatives contribute to the telling of stories about post-Euromaidan Ukraine to both domestic and international audiences. They belong to the three spheres of government, corporations, and civil society. In this chapter we focus on these three spheres and discuss some of the entities with a stake in the management of meaning in Ukraine, particularly those agents that are handling material in English for international audiences. To unpack the complex relations between these spheres, we use as our point of departure the Ministry of Information Policy, the Ukraine Crisis Media Center, and the PR agency CFC Consulting. These are not necessarily the most important entities, and they are certainly not the only ones, but they are clear and representative examples from government, civil society, and corporations. Even so, as we will show, the picture is far from clear-cut, and the boundaries between them are significantly blurred.

This account focuses on the managers of meaning inside Ukraine. Admittedly, there are agents with pretensions to form the image of Ukraine from abroad, such as international news media (e.g., the *Washington Post*, the

Guardian), diaspora organizations, investigative journalism groups (e.g., Bell-ingcat), and, of course, Russian media outlets (e.g., RT). These are, however, not among our examples. Our premise is that Russian aggression has engaged an entirely new set of actors in the management of information from the PR, journalism, corporate finance, and, most notably, voluntary sectors. These new actors bring competencies, ideologies, and practices from their respective fields, which impact the practice and expressive character of what is often termed information warfare. Importantly, they have cooperated with one another, and a pertinent question is how these managers of meaning relate to the state.

CONTESTED MANAGEMENT OF INFORMATION

In early 2015 the Ministry of Information Policy recruited Tetyana Popova, a high-profile media professional, as deputy minister. She had previously served as an adviser to the Ministry of Defense, and soon after joining the MIP she launched a government initiative to embed international journal-ists with the armed battalions fighting in the war zone of eastern Ukraine. This was a bold move that prompted an English-language business magazine to call her "Ukraine's Infowar Amazon" (*Business Ukraine* 2015). However, a year and a half later, she announced her resignation from the ministry, citing the government's failure to react to harassment and threats against journalists by right-wing groups (see, e.g., Hromadske TV 2016). The specific incident was a list published on certain websites containing the names and addresses of journalists who were accused of being "traitors" to Ukraine. The list included Popova herself.

When we contacted Popova in October 2016, a few months had passed since her resignation. We were interested in hearing about her experiences at the ministry and asked for a meeting during our next visit to Ukraine. We hoped she would now feel free to talk about her activities, having resigned from the MIP and no longer being perceived as representing the Ukrainian state. In a prompt reply she agreed and gave us a street address in Kyiv. It was widely known that she was now working as a senior strategy communica-tions expert with her own NGO Information Security, so we approached the address looking for something that resembled a typical office. Based on our previous meetings with several different NGOs, we were expecting Popova's to be housed in an ordinary apartment building. However, to our surprise, we found ourselves in front of a grand governmental building with a sign stating that it housed the Ministry of Information Policy.

We entered the building slightly confused and doubtful. Could we really convince the security staff that we had an appointment with a former deputy minister who had resigned over a major controversy with the government? But the middle-aged receptionist was remarkably facile. Neither he nor the young employee called to help us asked any questions about our business. We were informed that Popova was still at lunch, and we were kindly escorted up to the office floor to await her return. We realized that the ministry must be quite small, since there were not many people around. And we were puzzled by the relaxed attitude. We were obviously two noncitizens of Ukraine who did not speak or understand Ukrainian or Russian, but no one requested to see our identity papers or asked us to sign in to document the visit. And this was a government department in a country at war!

Popova arrived a few minutes later, and we were shown into her office. When we expressed our surprise about the location of our meeting, she explained that although she had resigned, a new deputy minister had not yet been appointed, and because the MIP still needed her services, she had agreed to make herself available. Thus, she continued to do the same job as previously, but now in the capacity of an adviser. Her basic responsibilities consisted of two projects: upgrading the technical equipment for broadcasting Ukrainian television in the war zones of Donetsk and Luhansk, and embedding journalists in the war zone. Both projects were explicitly regarded as a response to Russian efforts to control communications in and around the war zone. In a concrete sense, Popova was engaged in the management of meaning from a position at the MIP—whether formally employed by the government or not.

Popova said it had not been easy to convince the Ministry of Defense that foreign journalists should be allowed to accompany the military on the front lines. The Ministry of Defense was very conservative and much larger than the MIP, making it difficult to reform. However, after refusing three times, the ministry finally agreed, and Popova invited a group of journalists from both national and international media organizations to discuss how the project could be implemented. Using a contract developed by the US Army for its projects of embedding journalists with military personnel in war zones, such as in Iraq in 2009–2010, they adapted that to Ukrainian legislation with the help of a media lawyer.

Journalists would be allowed to accompany soldiers at the front lines under shelling, although the specific places varied according to the war situation. Each group of journalists could stay for a week, and if they were new to the country, they would be given an English-speaking press officer to guide them. It was, of course, very dangerous, Popova emphasized. In addition to signing the contract, the journalists had to obtain insurance, carry a pharmacy kit, and undergo training for a war zone. Still, she claimed, there had been no casualties among journalists taking part in the embedded program (although, at that time, at least eight journalists had been killed in other situations).

Popova acknowledged that her job, as well as the MIP's work in general, could be conceptualized as government propaganda. She was equally aware that it was controversial to embed journalists with one side engaged in a war. However, she insisted that the process of selecting journalists was completely transparent, and the application procedure for journalists who wanted to participate in the program was posted on the MIP's webpage. Popova claimed it was Ukrainian counterintelligence, not the MIP, that decided which applications to accept. In 2016 there were about four requests a month, and she showed us an information folder distributed to interested media organizations. It advised that applications for the embedded program should be sent "two weeks before the scheduled stay" to Popova's official email address at the ministry. Apparently, the former deputy minister was personally involved in assessing each request.

Popova was of the opinion that the program was working, although she had not yet formally evaluated the results. She referred, however, to the MIP's webpage, where a selection of news stories by embedded journalists had been uploaded. Altogether, there were links to forty-two articles from seventeen news organizations, including international platforms such as AFP (France); *Polsat* (Poland); the *Evening Standard Independent*, *Newsweek*, the *Telegraph*, and the *Times* (UK); and CNN and the *Huffington Post* (US). One week of embedding at the war front usually resulted in several stories. Most of them were rather long, describing in detail the lives of soldiers fighting from trenches and living in the basements of bombed houses. These stories were sad, Popova said, but "overall I think it is good for Ukraine. It shows that there is still shelling. People are dying. People are experiencing casualties."

It is not difficult to find reports from embedded journalists that Ukrainian authorities are probably very pleased with. In September 2015 the

Huffington Post, for example, published an article headlined "What It's Like on the Front Lines of the War in Ukraine" (Moldovan 2015). The story was written by a Romanian journalist—a member of one of the first embedded teams—in mid-August 2015. The reporter spent eight days with Ukrainian troops. The article describes one hot spot, near the destroyed Donetsk airport, where the landscape resembled "the set of an apocalypse movie." The reporter met soldiers whose "uniforms are so diverse that you don't see two alike from head to toe." The reason, the article explains, is that the Ukrainian army lacks the economic resources to equip its troops, so soldiers must obtain the necessary boots and clothes on their own or rely on what is donated by voluntary organizations.[1]

The soldiers in the *Huffington Post* story are called by their noms de guerre, for example, "Thunder," "Student," and "Zuzin." The latter was commander of the battalion hosting the reporter, and he was keen to tell the journalist that he was not fighting Ukrainian separatists or terrorists: "the first thing that he wants the world to know and remember is that the Russian Federation invaded Ukraine." Clearly, this message was consistent with the official Ukrainian view of the war: it was an invasion by Russian mercenaries, not a revolt by separatists.

But embedded journalists may not be completely reliable disseminators of the Ukrainian perspective. A reporter from the *Washington Post*, embedded at another hot spot close to Donetsk in August 2015, described a scenario very similar to the one in the *Huffington Post*. In the trench closest to the enemy's position stood the hallmark of this Ukrainian battalion: a massive Russian machine gun from 1930, still operational, that the soldiers called "the museum." Ukrainian troops obviously lacked resources, but the *Washington Post* reporter used this old machine gun as a metaphor—symbolizing not only the bad state of Ukrainian military equipment but also the soldiers' competence: "It's also unclear whether Ukrainian units . . . could handle high-end U.S. equipment. The troops here are a mixed bunch of professional soldiers and volunteers. When the company arrived on the front in March, 18 soldiers deserted when the fighting started" (Gibbons-Neff 2015).

The story thus took a turn that would probably not please an army commander. But does that mean it does not work in Ukraine's favor? Different agents might value this story differently. The Ukrainian army represents the traditional military power at the state's disposal, the institution with a monopoly on physical violence, and if the army cannot keep its personnel, this would be a major institutional problem. However, the MIP's other role was to manage the communicative power of Ukraine, and this did not always coincide with military logic.

Another MIP project was the iArmy, a small unit that handled the ministry's social media accounts and relayed mainly positive information about Ukraine on Facebook and Twitter. It also had a profile on Vkontakte (the Russian social networking service), but it was never very active, and in May 2017 Vkontakte was banned in Ukraine, along with a few other Russian websites. During our visit, Popova introduced us to the iArmy, which consisted of two young men in a small room, each of them sitting in front of a computer and reposting news stories. Its Facebook account Інформаційні війська України defined the iArmy as a community organization, and its web address was indeed @i.army.org. For the iArmy, stories about ill-equipped Ukrainian troops might not be unfavorable in terms of raising sympathy for the Ukrainian cause. The hard power of the military can thus be coupled with the soft communication power of meaning management.

SOFT INFORMATION POWER

When talking about her projects, Popova repeatedly referred to one predicament that constrained all the ministry's work: the limited economic resources available compared with Russia's finances. As an example, she mentioned RT (formerly known as Russia Today), the Russian state-controlled television channel that broadcasts news with a Russian perspective on the war to an international audience. Ukraine will never have such a large budget and needs be more realistic, she claimed. The project of embedding foreign journalists with Ukrainian troops was in fact an effort to influence international public opinion at minimal cost. In Popova's view, it is "much better to invite CNN, BBC, and the *Times* to the front line [and] locate them there for a week" than to influence the world with a Ukrainian version of RT.

By mentioning RT, Popova was obviously hinting at a Ukrainian satellite and online English-language television broadcaster aiming "to challenge the allegedly pro-Putin narrative of Russian state broadcasters" such as RT (Barber 2014).[2] Ukraine Today, or UT, was launched on Ukrainian Independence Day, 24 August 2014, under the motto "to inform, unite, and influence."[3] The phrase alludes to the motto formulated by John Reith (1924), the first general director of the BBC: "to inform, educate, and entertain." This motto has been the inspiration for many television and radio public service broadcasters in Euorpe (Langley 2014). UT, however, was not a public service broadcaster or even a state initiative. The television station was launched by the oligarch Ihor Kolomoysky. Although it was part of Kolomoysky's commercial 1+1 Media Group, the channel emphasized its political independence and nonprofit status: "Many volunteer initiatives launched in Ukraine with the aim of defending Ukraine and democracy from international aggression have become non-governmental organizations. Each organization has its specialty in fighting for the forces of good inside the hybrid war. Ukraine Today has also created a not-for-profit organization. Our mission is to win the battle against the abuse of information within the informational war" (quoted in Bolin, Jordan, and Ståhlberg 2016, 12).

In her assertion that the best way forward for Ukraine's information policy is to give Western media access, Popova is aligning with the basic principles of what Joseph Nye (2004) calls "soft power," that is, the ability to exercise symbolic power by "getting others to want the outcomes that you want" (Nye 2014, 20). Ukraine's relationship with the media is based on the conviction that if journalists get access, they will tell stories that serve the interests of Ukraine. One could argue that descriptions of the poor state of the Ukrainian army, with its randomly collected equipment and clothing, would undermine its authority. Alternatively, they might produce sympathy for the David in this battle against the Russian-supported, separatist Goliath and its much better equipped soldiers.

Nye's recipe for a successful engineering of soft power rests on three pillars: a country's culture, its political values, and the moral leadership of its foreign policy. It is mainly the latter two, and especially the third, that are relevant in this context. In a contest between David and Goliath, David will always have the moral sympathy. Importantly, however, Nye points to extrastate actors as the executioners of soft power, especially the cultural component. The culture of a nation needs to appeal to noncitizens and make them attracted to what they see. This is clearly difficult for a state ministry to arrange, indicating the limits of the state when it comes to soft power and public diplomacy. The project of embedding journalists is, in this sense, a kind of outsourcing of the management of meaning to commercial media organizations. Kolomoysky's Ukraine Today can be seen as another version of this tendency. As Nye states, information policy has indeed brought in other actors: "Governments," he says, "will remain the most powerful actors on the global stage. However, the stage will become more crowded, and many non-state actors will compete effectively for influence" (2014, 20). In Ukraine, these extrastate actors could be both commercial and noncommercial, and they are often intricately intertwined with government activities.

The fact that state ministries, civil society organizations, and NGOs are involved in forming Ukraine's image might be seen as a strategy for coordinating the many actors on the stage Nye describes. In this light, it is only logical that people like Tetyana Popova are seamlessly moving between an NGO and the MIP. The former deputy minister is perhaps the most telling case: she has quit her government job but is still doing the same work, even sitting in the same office. The only difference is that she is now an adviser to the government while employed by an NGO. And she is not the only example in Ukraine of how the boundaries between governmental and nongovernmental actors are blurring. This blurring of boundaries is also evident in other MIP activities, which often include the involvement of the business or the voluntary sector. It is also seen in the labeling of the ministry's own subdivision—iArmy's .org web address indicating civil society status.

This governmental cooperation with civil society organizations and corporate businesses is openly declared by the ministry itself. On its webpage, the logotypes of some well-known Ukrainian NGOs engaged in debunking news stories and countering negative information about Ukraine are prominently displayed: Detector Media, InformNapalm, and StopFake.[4] This cooperation is also indicated by the MIP's limited staff, which means it must rely on extensive collaboration with external, nongovernmental actors to maintain its operations. This situation can also be considered in the historical light of the Soviet legacy, where civil society organizations were closely related to the state. Even if Soviet NGOs were an integral part of the state's activities to an extent not found in Ukraine after Euromaidan, the blurring of boundaries can find a historical explanation here. Perhaps equally, an explanation can be found among neoliberal tendencies for outsourcing state responsibilities. To more fully understand the relations involved in meaning management in Ukraine, the next section looks more closely at the Ukraine Crisis Media Center, formed by private initiative shortly after the Euromaidan Revolution and managing communication among international journalists as well as on a domestic level.

THE MANAGEMENT OF STATE COMMUNICATION BY CIVIL SOCIETY

The Ukraine Crisis Media Center was set up in March 2014 in the wake of the violent and tumultuous events in Kyiv between late November and February. Established in Hotel Ukraine at the top of Maidan Nezalezhnosti, the UCMC's primary purpose was to assist foreign correspondents reporting the latest developments of the Ukraine war. The hotel had already been prominently displayed around the world as film footage captured those turbulent months of street protests and fights. Bullet holes in the façade testified to the presence of snipers shooting at nearby protesters. Later, the UCMC moved to the Ukrainian House, a conference hall just one block from Maidan.

The UCMC provided a platform for the government, with daily briefings, press conferences, and press releases issued by army spokespersons and civil society alike. When the war in the east started in the summer of 2014, it was on the third floor of Hotel Ukraine that journalists were briefed about battles and casualties. For journalists on assignment in Ukraine, Colonel Andriy Lysenko soon became an important face, as he appeared regularly at 1:00 p.m. on weekdays with new details of troop movements and casualties (figure 2.1). The colonel spoke in Ukrainian, but the UCMC provided headphones with simultaneous translations in English. The army briefings as well as all other sessions were filmed and posted on the internet each day. Tetyana Popova, then working as an adviser to the Ministry of Defense, was one of the people who facilitated this cooperation between the army and the UCMC.

The UCMC directed its activities toward providing information to international journalists covering the situation in Ukraine—activities that are typically the government's responsibility. The founders of the UCMC, however, were entrepreneurs from the PR industry, backed by funding from a number of European and American organizations. One was Vasyl Myroshnychenko, a PR consultant at the Kyiv-based marketing and PR agency CFC Consulting. This professional background is important to an understanding of how the UCMC contributes to managing meaning in the aftermath of the Euromaidan Revolution.

Myroshnychenko and his partner Gennadiy Kurochka founded CFC Consulting in 2002. One of their first large projects was to arrange Ukraine's participation in the Eurovision Song Contest in 2003 and again in 2004, when they promoted popular singer Ruslana, who won the competition and thus secured Ukraine's position as the next year's host country. They

Figure 2.1
Colonel Andriy Lysenko at a press briefing at UCMC, 17 November 2014.
Photo by authors.

also orchestrated the publicity when Ukraine hosted the ESC final in Kyiv in 2005 (see Bolin 2006b). Kurochka and Myroshnychenko described their involvement in the ESC as a way to promote Ukraine's international image. CFC's involvement in selecting the Ukrainian representative at the ESC demonstrates that participation in such media events is controlled by a small elite circle that decides and disseminates what constitutes national culture in Ukraine and promotes that message to the rest of Europe.[5]

The ESC is not the only effort CFC made to "put Ukraine on the map." It approached international television broadcasters such as CNN, BBC World, and Euronews and requested that they include Ukraine on their weather charts: "They showed this map at least five to six times a day, and when people of Europe looked at it, they probably thought that Ukraine did not exist, like no people were living here. So, we sent some faxes and told them we are a country in Europe with 45 million people, and why don't you add some cities in Ukraine and get at least the weather in Kyiv?" (Myroshnychenko interview,

May 2013). The lobbying was at least partially effective, as Euronews added Ukraine to its weather forecasts.

CFC thus had some experience producing soft information policy on behalf of Ukraine as a nation-state, and the initiative to launch the UCMC was a logical continuation of this. The actual establishment of the UCMC resulted from a collaboration between Kurochka and colleague Natalia Popovych, president of the PR agency PRP, also based in Kyiv. PRP engaged in brand management, crisis communications, and corporate and social responsibility services, according to its now-defunct website.[6] Like Kurochka and Myroshnychenko, Popovych's motivation for launching the UCMC was to improve the international perception of Ukraine, but also "to counter Russian propaganda, which is very powerful" (Popovych, personal communication, June 2014). Russian propaganda is frequently mentioned in interviews with the key actors involved with the UCMC. According to Myroshnychenko, "there are still a number of people who are to a great deal influenced by the Russian propaganda, which is very heavily present here" (personal communication, November 2014). All three key actors have taken an increasingly patriotic approach to the developments following Euromaidan. For example, when Vladimir Putin was addressing the United Nations General Assembly in New York in 2015, Kurochka and Popovych unfurled a torn, ragged, and bullet-riddled Ukrainian flag salvaged from the eastern front, a spectacular coup that got the attention of the international news media (Sukhov 2015). After all, they are PR professionals and know how to stand out in a media landscape permeated with messages. They have taken advantage of these skills repeatedly, as noted below.

Even after the Euromaidan events and their turbulent aftermath had disappeared from the headlines, the UCMC continued its briefings, press conferences, and practical assistance to foreign journalists covering Ukraine. However, as a communication platform, the UCMC has changed since its start in 2014. As foreign reporters' interest moved to other hot spots of conflict around the world, the daily news briefings and other press center activities decreased. The daily schedule became sparser over the years and was shifting toward Ukrainian civil society rather than international audiences. This, of course, changed with the Russian invasion in early 2022, when many of the UCMC's activities were revived.

One of the UCMC's major projects since 2016 has been the Hybrid Warfare Analytical Group (HWAG), which is devoted to "detecting and deconstructing Russian influence operations, improving government's strategic communications and building resilience towards malign influence."[7] The HWAG has collaborated with forty partner organizations in Ukraine as well as internationally; among the latter are the Renaissance and Fulbright Foundations, US Department of State, North Atlantic Treaty Organization (NATO), and Organization for Security and Co-operation in Europe (OSCE). Whereas the initial aim of the UCMC was to supply international media outlets with information about the Ukrainian situation—from a Ukrainian point of view—the HWAG's activities are different. It has been monitoring how Russian state-controlled mass media produce and disseminate deceptive images and narratives of Ukraine, Europe, and the US. These Russian communications are understood to consist of propaganda and disinformation. The HWAG's findings have been published as reports, presentations, and videos published on Facebook and disseminated through dedicated social media profiles.[8]

Gradually, the UCMC has become an organization that produces content as well as serving as a press center and a platform for civil society and state authorities. With the HWAG, its activities are closely related to a number of other actors engaged in detecting and analyzing disinformation about Ukraine. StopFake, mentioned previously, is one of the UCMC's domestic partners. In addition, there are several other specialized organizations in Ukraine, such as Detector Media, InformNapalm, Voxcheck, and Internews Ukraine, as well as news media platforms such as Euromaidan Press, that monitor disinformation and propaganda. What these organizations all have in common is that they are NGOs, formally independent from Ukrainian state authorities. The government does not have a similar entity engaging in such activities, although it announced in late 2020 that such a center will be launched (Tsybulska 2020). The NGOs do, however, cooperate with ministries or government departments and occasionally act together to influence government policies. They are not afraid of criticizing or confronting the Ukrainian government. For example, when the new president Volodymir Zelenski was elected in 2019, a large number of NGOs with a common mission to "protect the values that Ukrainians fought for during the Revolution of Dignity" made a joint statement of "red lines not to be crossed" under his presidency. The "red lines" included detailed instructions regarding both foreign policy and media and information policies.[9]

Core individuals who are active in these organizations often know one another well. They frequently have similar professional or educational backgrounds and have sometimes worked together in other professional roles. Upon meeting activists in these various NGOs, it became apparent that they often have ambivalent relationships with Ukrainian government institutions. On the one hand, they perceive their activism as supportive of the Ukrainian government; on the other hand, their trust in state authorities is often very low.

The fact that many of these agents have complex personal relationships and serve in different roles means that it is not always easy to identify the origin of initiatives for information management. It is often unclear whether a particular project started in civil society, among private entrepreneurs, or on the initiative of the state. Several individuals involved in the UCMC actually represent both civic and corporate engagement in the management of meaning in Ukraine. As we followed specific cases of such management during our fieldwork in Ukraine, we came to understand how efforts to communicate meaning about Ukraine have been initiated by private individuals who then approached state departments to launch their ideas, which were either turned down or became the object of tenders.

THE MANAGEMENT OF STATE COMMUNICATION
BY CORPORATE AGENTS

So far, we have described the intertwining of the MIP as an institution of the state with civil society agents in the form of NGOs. This entanglement can be somewhat confusing, as in the case of Tetyana Popova, who is representing an NGO but acting as a deputy minister, or, conversely, an in-house iArmy acting as an NGO. We have also shown that the UCMC, an NGO with strong links to the corporate sector, has had an important role in managing meaning about Ukraine and about Russian aggression. To highlight the close connection to the corporate sector, a short description of the procedures surrounding nation branding campaigns is illustrative. This account also brings in commercial actors such as CFC Consulting involved in both branding and conflict communication.

In our earlier writings, we defined nation branding as "the practice of governments in conjunction with public relations consultants and corporate business to launch campaigns promoting a certain image of the nation-state"

(Bolin and Ståhlberg 2015, 3065). This is also how nation branding is generally perceived in scholarly writing about the phenomenon (e.g., Aronczyk 2008, 42; Kaneva 2011, 118). However, nation branding campaigns do not always begin within the state administration; nor do they grow from ideas cultivated in parliaments. Rather, they often originate among professionals in the PR and advertising industries, who need to create a demand for their services (Bolin and Ståhlberg 2021). This demand is created step by step by convincing politicians and state administrators of the need to "put the country on the map," just as PR agents at CFC convinced Euronews to report the weather in Ukraine. With this success story in its back pocket, CFC could approach the Ukrainian government and argue that the country needed more international visibility.

In Ukraine and elsewhere, advertising and PR work on the basis of market dynamics. If we compare the branding market with the market for ordinary consumer items such as soap, toothpaste, and other mass-produced goods that come in multiple brands and require product differentiation, we can see the principal difference between them. While the ordinary market for consumer goods is based on demand, which producers exploit to their benefit, in the market for brands, the producer has to manufacture not only the commodity (the brand) but also the demand for it. And the demand for nation branding does not grow organically; it must be produced. If we compare it with the market for food, for example, there is no basic need that the brand commodity is supposed to satisfy: "A commodity," as Karl Marx ([1867] 1976) defines it, "is, in the first place, an object outside us, a thing that by its properties satisfies human wants of some sort or another. The nature of such wants, whether, for instance, they spring from the stomach or from fancy, makes no difference." It is quite clear that the "wants" the brand is supposed to satisfy have their origin in fancy rather than in the stomach. But such fancy does not arrive by itself.

Moreover, the effects of PR are extremely hard to measure—not least because one never knows what would have happened in the absence of an advertising campaign. Accordingly, a belief in the success of a branding campaign has to be produced and its efficacy proved. Most often, proof of success is anecdotal—for example, based on the fact that a television broadcaster has started to report the weather in Kyiv. Furthermore, as Melissa Aronczyk (2013) has shown in her research on campaigns in North America and Europe, the evaluation of success is most often made by the same people who orchestrated the campaign.

Branding agencies have to propose campaigns to politicians if they want to be commissioned to execute the actual campaign. In the words of Pierre Bourdieu, just like other discourse-producing agents such as poets, intellectuals, and lawmakers, branding agencies have to "produce the imaginary referent in the name of which they speak" ([2012] 2020, 63). The tools used to convince politicians often take the form of a brand book, a presentation, or a stack of PowerPoint slides. Branding agencies produce these presentational media on speculation, hoping to create demand for their services.

The branding market is complex, with an intricate web of relations among different types of vendors and customers. Those who sell advertising, for example, do not sell their ads to the consumer of the branded commodity; they work as an intermediary between the client—often a seller of goods—and the consumer of those goods, trying to convince the customer to buy the client's product rather than someone else's. The nation branding market works differently because the client of the branding company does not actually sell anything other than the general reputation of the country in question. Those who benefit economically are the hospitality and tourism industries, rather than the governmental agency that is the branding company's client. Those who pay the bill for the PR agencies' services are not the ones that produce the commodities sold or the services delivered, and they are not the ones to receive the revenue from increased financial investment (except for a possible increase in tax revenue). If we consider the definition of nation branding mentioned earlier—an activity that involves "governments in conjunction with public relations consultants and corporate business"—we can conclude that even if there is cooperation among these partners, initiatives rarely come from governments; they come from the advertising and PR sector.

These types of public-private enterprises are, however, politically sensitive. Large nation branding campaigns are expensive if one includes preparations, research in the form of focus group interviews with potential audiences, design work, organizational work, and so forth. For countries with unstable economies such as Ukraine and many other post-Soviet countries, spending millions on advertising campaigns that may be controversial in the eyes of the domestic population is problematic and can easily backfire. Financing is thus often channeled through foundations launched for this single purpose. When Estonia launched its Brand Estonia campaign in relation to the Eurovision Song Contest in 2002, it also created the foundation Enterprise Estonia (Bolin 2002; Jordan 2014b). In Ukraine, the corresponding institution was the Ukraine

Economic Reform Fund (Bolin and Ståhlberg 2015). Ukraine's Ministry of Foreign Affairs invested a minor sum in the project—the amount differs, based on who is being interviewed, from US$100,000 to US$250,000—and a much larger sum was provided by the Economic Reform Fund, which meant that it bypassed the state budget. Whether these finances originated from the state or from private business is unclear.

As a form of information policy, then, nation branding integrates corporate initiative and state funding, often via institutions semidetached from the state with names such as Enterprise Estonia or the Ukraine Economic Reform Fund. The latter is a private initiative for sponsoring projects aimed at improving Ukraine's image abroad for tourists and investors, but it also claims to be working closely with the government (see Bolin and Ståhlberg 2015, 3073ff.). These types of organizations blur the distinction between state, civil society, and corporate business. The state-business relation is not unique to Ukraine and can certainly be found elsewhere. In Sweden, for example, tours of large Swedish corporations such as Volvo, IKEA, and ASEA have long been part of state visits, as well as meetings with the Swedish royal family, presumably based on the principle that what is good for large Swedish-owned transnational corporations is good for Sweden. What might be unique in the Ukrainian case in the wake of Euromaidan are the blurred lines between civil society and the state, and the mixture of all three societal spheres might in fact be characteristic of postcommunist countries such as the Soviet Union and of communist China. Arguably, this blurring of societal spheres can be explained historically and can be seen in the light of how civil society organizations were integrated with the state during communist times, when they were effectively part of the party-state system of the USSR (Aliyev 2015). This fact might explain the low levels of trust in both state and civil society institutions in postcommunist central and eastern Europe (see, e.g., Bakardjieva et al. 2021). However, it might also explain the blurred boundaries between state institutions and the institutions of civil society, including NGOs, as the line between them was indistinct from the start.

THE BLURRED BOUNDARIES OF THE INFORMATIONAL STATE

The managers of meaning described earlier represent the three spheres of the state, civil society, and corporations. The examples of the Ministry of Information Policy, the Ukraine Crisis Media Center, and the various PR agents provoke questions about the Ukrainian state and its informational functions. But how can we think of the state as an administrative and political entity in this context? What kind of state is post-Euromaidan Ukraine, and what are its agents? On what powers does it rest, and what are the roles of the MIP and the other agents involved in policy formation?

In his lectures on the state, Bourdieu argues that the state has a specific position as an absolute power. He expands, or perhaps makes more precise, Max Weber's famous definition of the state as the institution with a monopoly of physical violence by adding *symbolic violence*—that is, control over the resources to represent social realities (Bourdieu [2012] 2020, 4). As Monroe Price (2015, 4) stresses, the power over violence, as well as the power over communication and information flows, can be delegated. And if we think of the state as the entity that controls both physical and symbolic violence within a certain territory, what roles do the different agents involved in the management of information play? How should the post-Euromaidan Ukrainian state be theorized in relation to previous formations of the state? To answer this question, we need to situate the present Ukrainian state in the longer history of state formation.

As Sandra Braman (2006, 28ff.) points out with clarity in her broad historical overview of the types of state formation, the informational state historically succeeds the bureaucratic state and the bureaucratic welfare state. The informational state is networked, and it integrates state ministries and administrations with nonstate actors in a system characterized by "multiple interdependencies . . . in ways that largely require use of the global information infrastructure for information creation, processing, flows, and use" (Braman 2006, 36). Ned Rossiter makes a similar observation, arguing that an organized network "must engage, by necessity, other institutional partners who may often be opposed to their interests" (2006, 36). In a way, this is a seemingly accurate description of the interrelations among actors as they are described in this chapter, and it would be seen as a type of "multistakeholderism" were it not for the fact that the activities lack the "degree of centralization and hierarchization . . . essential for a network to be characterized as organized" (Rossiter 2006, 49). This, then, is not so much about the delegation of state functions but rather about a set of unorganized parallel activities. However, Ukraine is a specific kind of informational state, not only because the government's information resources are severely hampered by its much better resourced Russian neighbor but also because of the government's reliance on civil society organizations, making NGOs and corporate agents much more prominent than in countries such as Sweden, France, Germany, or Braman's main example, the US.

Interrelations between such "complex adaptive systems," as Braman (2006, 36) calls the agents involved, is inherently dependent on the affordances of communication technologies. The informational state is thus formed *in* communication, to paraphrase John Dewey (1916, 5), although he was writing about society in its entirety, not only the state. This means that the differences between state formations, just as the differences between societies, are based not on any quantitative informational or communicative difference but on a qualitative difference. Different communication technologies privilege different ways of communicating and have different abilities to provide for "information creation, processing, flows, and use" (Braman 2006, 36), which then define the specific society—or state. The qualitative differences between informational states over time are thus colored by the specific dynamics of the media and communications technologies, the practices developed around their use, and the combination of agents involved.

These qualitative differences can also be discerned among different informational states, and one of the conclusions of this chapter is that the Ukrainian informational state is configured in a specific way. It is more fluid than other informational states, and the boundaries between its agents are more blurred. An important feature of Ukrainian policy management is the influx of people in the political administration with backgrounds in PR and advertising or who work in close collaboration with people from that sector. At times, there have also been very strong links between corporate power and oligarchs and the political system, including business relationships as well as social and family relationships (Åslund 2014). It can thus be difficult to judge in what role specific agents appear in different situations: are they representing the state, an NGO, or a private enterprise?

When we first started to identify and map actors involved in managing meaning about Ukraine, we cast our net widely, trying to include various types of agents and a broad spectrum of practices. As the list of organizations and individuals grew, it became clear that we needed to make distinctions among the different kinds of agents, but it was not obvious how to make simple, one-dimensional distinctions. That list, which soon included some fifty organizations or groups that were managing meaning for an international audience, could be reshuffled in several ways. We could, for example, make distinctions between governmental, commercial, and voluntary organizations, but as explained earlier, as we learned more about these actors, it became harder to pin down how each agent should be characterized. Alternatively, we could make conventional distinctions between mass media organizations or types of information-related work—for example, grouping news producers, TV channels, radio stations, news bureaus, PR consultants, think tanks, and groups involved in surveillance and analysis—regardless of whether an organization was governmental, commercial, or voluntary. The latter distinctions revealed some interesting patterns. For example, the number of actors involved in surveillance and analysis grew steadily and, after a few years, became almost as numerous as those producing or distributing news in English. Most striking, however, was that this type of categorization was of little use, simply because the agents could seldom be described as stable entities in terms of either their organization or their communication activities and use of media technologies.

What we see in Ukraine is not only a blurring of boundaries between organizational forms—between state, market, and voluntary organizations. It is also a blurring of boundaries between types of meaning-making activities—that is, what exactly the various organizations are working with. Initially, when we started to follow the situation in Ukraine, it was possible to see a pattern of complementarity in the activities of various organizations. Soon after the Euromaidan events, newly formed groups created to counter Russian propaganda seemed to take on different roles and contributed with special competence to the overall task. For example, Hromadske TV and Euromaidan Press were producing and distributing media content through television, the internet, and social media; the UCMC was offering services to foreign media correspondents and a platform for domestic civil society; and StopFake was monitoring mass media and debunking "fake news" about Ukraine. It seemed evident that none of these organizations alone could fulfill the goal of countering Russian propaganda. Their different activities were specialized and complementary, and the NGOs seemed almost like discrete departments of a large, somewhat informally organized, and loosely coordinated company contributing to a common objective (Bolin, Jordan, and Ståhlberg 2016).

This pattern of mutually complementary relations became much less prominent over the years. The main organizations involved in meaning management related to the Ukrainian situation started new projects and activities, while other commitments were discontinued or declined in importance. The core function of each actor became less obvious. Activities often overlapped. For example, the UCMC not only offers press center facilities but also monitors Russian media and produces its own content (e.g., texts, videos, posters, analyses, reports). StopFake has become involved in domestic media literacy projects and also devotes considerable time to international fact-checking seminars and collaborations. It is no longer just debunking factual inaccuracies in the Russian news media. Euromaidan Press produces video manuals on how to detect propaganda, but it also organizes photo exhibitions on the war in Donbas, as well as providing news from Ukraine in English.

One obvious reason for this blurring of boundaries is that the ecology of Ukrainian meaning-management organizations is not analogous to the departments of a large corporation. There is no central board that coordinates roles and activities; the MIP is certainly not in a position to exert power over other interested parties in their endeavor to manage meaning. Consequently, each organization follows its own rationales and develops and transforms accordingly. Formally independent NGOs may take on new projects that freely make use of the ideas, skills, and social networks of their members and staff.

Importantly, however, NGO work must be funded. Money usually comes from public funding, corporate sponsors, or fundraising projects that attract private donors. International development organizations and foreign states are also major contributors to local NGOs around the world. The post-Euromaidan situation in Kyiv since 2014 has indeed attracted substantial attention from American and European funding bodies. The larger Ukrainian NGOs present impressive lists of foreign sponsors and donors related to specific European and American state authorities (embassies and foreign ministries of neighboring states in particular), the European Union (through bodies such as the European Endowment for Democracy), and international nongovernmental funding organizations (e.g., the International Renaissance Foundation). Anthropologist Taras Fedirko has described this constellation as "a loose bloc of liberal civil society organisations (constituted predominantly by Western-funded policy-oriented think-tanks, watchdog and activist organisations), with sections of middle-class professionals, intelligentsia and entrepreneurs" (2021, 474).

A Ukrainian NGO might very well engage in new projects because its leading members and staff find them worthwhile or interesting, but it still has to apply for funding with proposals that conform to donors' priorities. Projects that monitor and analyze dubious media content or raise awareness about propaganda seem to be popular among major international donors.

Moreover, Ukrainian groups are often part of international networks of organizations and individuals that share resources and skills, such as Open Information Partnership. In that sense, the Ukrainian practice of countering Russian propaganda is interlaced with a transnational perspective on information policy. Thus, the field of meaning management in Ukraine is not a closed system; Ukrainian actors are very much a part of the transnational culture concerned with the construction and well-being of nation-states (Boli and Thomas 1999).

How does this blurring of boundaries influence our perspective of the Ukrainian state? Obviously, it takes us very far from conventional views of the state as a monolithic entity equipped with a bureaucratic apparatus that effectively upholds power and controls essential societal functions. This view dominates in both scholarship and commonsense discourse about state policy in general and propaganda in particular. It is also revealed in descriptions of the aggressors through metonyms such as *Kremlin, Moscow*, and even *Putin*. According to this view, the state decides what to do and how to act, and it has a voice and agency of its own. Weber's characterization of the state as an entity with a monopoly of physical violence and Bourdieu's expanded understanding that includes symbolic power are based on a view of the state as an integrated and reified agent. In his lectures on biopolitics, Michel Foucault (2007) shares this idea of the state as a strong unified actor that exerts control over populations through particular means and instruments such as statistics. This is not what we have observed in Ukraine.

There are, however, alternative perspectives that dispute the state as a unitary, taken-for-granted entity. One such perspective is world polity institutionalism, which views the nation-state as constructed and embedded within a worldwide culture of organizations and policies, rather than as a rational collective actor grounded in local history and politics. In this macrophenomenological perspective, worldwide models—for example, of justice, equality, and economic development—define the actions of local actors and shape the agendas and policies of nation-states (Meyer et al. 1997). Considering that all the actors we studied are managing information for an international audience and many of them are also closely interacting with (and often funded by) international organizations, this perspective is relevant.

However, our methodological approach also brings this study close to a more micro-oriented critique of the state as a rational actor. Akhil Gupta, for example, argues that: "Scholars, no less than policymakers, are prone to making authoritative pronouncements about the nature of the state, its intention, its capacities, and its abilities to deliver on its promises, and so forth. I think of such claims to knowledge as illegitimate, not because they intentionally set out to reify the state but because they do so by default" (2012, 53). Gupta is an anthropologist and makes his critical point from an empirical position. He insists that scholars should specify what they mean when referring to "the state." Do they mean central, regional, or local state authorities? What branch of administration and what policies, programs, or people are they studying? Gupta has studied the lowest rung of state bureaucracies in India, and from that position, an alternative picture emerges. Instead of the extremely isomorphic world of nation-states that world polity institutionalists envision, he sees barely controlled chaos and arbitrariness (Gupta 2012, 14). As shown in the chapters that follow, this view has resonance in our material.

CONCLUSION

In this chapter we accounted for and discussed the various domestic agents with a stake in managing the image of Ukraine presented to an external audience. They can all be found within the three spheres of the state, the corporate sector, and civil society. Rather than providing an exhaustive account, our aim was to cite illustrative examples that point to the fluid nature of these spheres. Based on this account, we can conclude that the boundaries between various agents involved in information and meaning management are not clear-cut. There is a substantial overlap in their activities, and some individuals tend to move between corporate and governmental sectors and civil society organizations.

Although we share Gupta's view that the state as a singular, homogeneous entity is not an object that can be studied, it is a representation produced by powerful or influential interests through prodigious cultural work and media technologies. Thus, a coherent and purposeful state should not be a point of departure; rather, the analytical problem requiring explanation is how the state is represented as such (Gupta 2012, 57ff.). This is what studies of nationalism or nation branding are all about. How is a population and a territory produced—as an imagined community or as an imagined commodity? As we have argued elsewhere (Bolin and Ståhlberg 2021), this is also our perspective on meaning management in Ukraine during turbulent times. Rather than a state acting as a coherent entity in a propaganda war, a large number of agents with an unclear relation to state authorities are trying to represent Ukraine as a legitimate entity through cultural work that could be characterized as chaotic and arbitrary but is also in tune with transnational ideas of information policy. In the next chapter we look at how this is done, in which forms, and with what kinds of media technologies.

FORMS AND ASSEMBLAGES

Today's mass media is tomorrow's fossil fuel.
—Michael Crichton (1993)

To produce a narrative is to attempt to create coherence among events, individuals, places, and contexts—it is about creating meaningful connections between seemingly disparate things, to order the world in a meaningful way by assigning causal relations to textual elements. If one wants to convey a meaningful message to a recipient, this is a basic rule of thumb. Things that are not perceived as meaningful are often ignored. In a world where there is an abundance of stories, images, and events scrolling by, it is easy for messages to drown in the flood of signs that permeate the media landscapes of modern life. The task of the professional communicator is thus to manage information—signs—in ways that are perceived as meaningful to the relevant target group. What every professional and strategic communicator intends, of course, is to steer minds in certain directions—to provoke desire for a specific commodity (product branding) or country or region (place or nation branding) or to portray a certain way of life as attractive (soft power). To produce narratives that are intended to be attractive, meaningful, and relevant is to be in the business of "the formation of men's [sic] attitudes" (Ellul 1965). Whether these narratives are perceived as meaningful is an empirical question that we put aside in this chapter to focus on the means and forms by which narratives and other assemblages of meaning are constructed. However, not all information comes in narrative form. In fact, we question whether the narrative is the only, or even the most dominant, form of meaning management in the contemporary media landscape.

The previous chapter discussed some of the agents involved in the management of information in Ukraine and the blurring of the boundaries between the different types of organizations that serve as their communications bases.

In this chapter we take a more in-depth look at some of the communication tools and channels adopted by these agents in the attempt to manage meaning in post-Euromaidan Ukraine. Which communications platforms do they employ? What technologies, genres, and representational forms are used to manage communication? In a plural media landscape, information of various kinds travels rapidly between media technologies. Naturally, the traditional mass media are important for the construction and circulation of meaning, but other media forms, rooted in other media technologies, often precede mass media stories. Narrative structures and stylistic elements are formed in brand manuals, communication plans, PowerPoint slides, outdoor advertising, event marketing, street art, and, not least, niche media such as live-streamed television and online "spreadable media" such as Facebook, Twitter, and VKontakte before they reach international audiences (Jenkins, Ford, and Green 2013).

The means of narrative construction are found both in the frameworks of knowledge in which narratives appear (e.g., the genre system), or narrative conventions, and in the technical infrastructures—the actual media technologies by which narratives are assembled and distributed. In today's media-saturated landscapes, there is a plurality of media platforms that can be used for informational purposes, run by various types of organizations. This means that images and signs flow through a range of media technologies, and the presentational forms are remediated and molded in various ways before they are interpreted among general audiences (Bolter and Grusin 2000). However, they are not always molded as narratives. Rather, most signs and images are circulating as fragments or incomplete narrative elements. Snippets of heterogeneous information may also be collected and circulated as assemblages of meaning that lack the coherence and temporal form of a narrative. They can be considered preforms of narratives or just plain discourse—that is, a way of talking about a certain subject.

In this chapter we trace these preforms and discuss their role in the management of meaning. We show how the images and perceptions underlying policy narratives and branding stories are molded in various media technologies and presentational forms that have their own specific affordances and presentational biases, which are then exported to the mass media images and stories that eventually reach broader audiences and publics. Within a framework of media theory, we discuss how specific media technologies and texts impact the management of information. Previous research on opinion formation and persuasion often focused too narrowly on traditional genres such as news and journalism as sources of influence, which put those genres at the center of policy debates (e.g., the widespread discourse on "fake news"). We argue that we need to dig more deeply into what Stuart Hall (1973) calls the "encoding moment" of communication to understand how images of countries and regions are structured in communication. We need to see in more detail how texts come into being as meaningful assemblages.

In the next section, we briefly examine how news and information came to be used as vehicles of influence, propaganda, and opinion based in mass media technologies, followed by a discussion of the encoding moment of communication and how texts, images, and narratives become remediated and circulated in this moment. Our argument is that the way communication is theorized is tightly coupled with contemporary media technologies, and we need to keep that historical perspective in mind when analyzing how messages come into being in the present. The main part of the chapter uses two examples to show how narratives and textual components circulate between media technologies and media forms in the contemporary landscape of mass, niche, and social media. The first example offers glimpses into the encoding moments around the Euromaidan events and discusses how messages are formed, remediated, and circulated between social media, niche and online communication technologies, and mass media. The second case exemplifies how remediation and circulation take shape in the process of branding campaigns. In this case, the circulation of information and the message's textual features are related in less obvious ways and are harder to observe, as the circulation is not always publicly accessible. Here, we focus on presentational media such as PowerPoint to show how images, texts, and messages are remixed and reshuffled in various combinations before they eventually appear in the mass media. Our argument is that the open-ended form of presentational media takes advantage of discursive elements and narrative components without producing any stable or unified story that reaches a narrative closure. A presentational medium is a technology that offers assemblages of meaning rather than narratives.

FROM POWERFUL MEDIA EFFECTS TO THE CIRCULATION OF MEANING

Throughout history, the introduction of each new media technology has been followed by fears of the power of that technology. During the Middle Ages, when books were reproduced by hand and only a few copies existed, some books that were considered very dangerous were not allowed to be read and were hidden away in libraries—as vividly described in Umberto Eco's bestseller *The Name of the Rose* ([1980] 1994). Although texts were limited, they were also powerful. Recall that propaganda as a concept has its roots in early modern Europe, stemming from Ignatius of Loyola, the Jesuits, and subsequently the committee of cardinals founded by Pope Gregory XV to propagate the true faith of the Catholic Church.

Garth Jowett and Victoria O'Donnell give detailed accounts of the preforms of modern propaganda and show that the printing press allowed the dissemination of critical leaflets against the Catholic Church during the Reformation and was a prerequisite for Martin Luther when he translated the German-language Bible in 1534. The printing of the Bible in vernacular language was an important challenge to the Roman Catholic Church, but it was accompanied by the printing of satirical woodcuts by skilled artists such as Lucas Cranach (Jowett and O'Donnell 1992, 48ff.). In the history of art, ideological accounts are legion, and kings and emperors have been portrayed in a favorable light, but only with the appearance of the mass press in the nineteenth century did images and texts of an openly propagandistic nature become widespread throughout society.

The printing press was the first technology that allowed the multiplication of identical texts; this increased the number of copies available, in turn paving the way for a more plural textual landscape. One could say that the development of propaganda followed the development of communication technologies. With the establishment of the mass press and then cinema toward the end of the nineteenth century, a tight relationship developed among journalism, opinion formation, and propaganda, along with a great expansion in propaganda activities (Jowett and O'Donnell 1992, 79). This means that propaganda should be related to other forms of mass communication directed at political opinion formation and persuasion and should be seen as a major part of twentieth-century mass communications research (Glander 2000). The rise of the mass press and the cinema led to the mass audience and an increased interest in the psychology of the masses and how they could be manipulated. Gustave Le Bon ([1896] 2006), Hugo Münsterberg (1916), and others theorized the psychological dimensions of this manipulation, based on the assumption that the masses are gullible and that the media's "penetrating influence must be fraught with dangers" (Münsterberg 1916, 221).

Over the course of the twentieth century, propaganda research was relegated to the background of mainstream media and communications research, leading to a more pronounced focus on opinion formation. Political opinion formation has gradually become a major field within political communication studies, and over the years, several important mass communication models have been introduced, such as Elihu Katz and Paul Lazarsfeld's (1955) two-step communication flow, as well as theories on public opinion in the wake of Walter Lippmann ([1922] 1946) and later theories such as Maxwell McCombs and Donald Shaw's (1972) agenda-setting theory of the media.

Research on opinion formation and media influence has, however, concentrated on news as the main format to be analyzed. This is strange, given that early research had much broader perspectives and considered influences from several media forms and genres. Harold Lasswell ([1927] 1971), for example, gives plenty of examples of books and films that served as propaganda in the early decades of the twentieth century. We should bear in mind that, before the introduction of television in the 1950s, cinema was not only an entertainment medium; newsreels were important sources of news for many people. And Katz and Lazarsfeld (1955), in their important study *Personal Influence*, substantially expanded examples of influence beyond political opinion formation to include the formation of fashion.

In a similar manner, Jacques Ellul's work on propaganda and persuasion takes a broader approach. Importantly, however, he rejects simple definitions of propaganda as a tool for transforming opinions and instead argues that its pupose is no longer to modify ideas but "to arouse an active and mythical belief" (Ellul 1965, 25). Propaganda, he says, is not about misinformation and lies—"truth," he argues, "is an inappropriate term here" (52). It is more in line with political education, in that it produces a Weltanschauung—an approach to the world, or a way of perceiving things and practices from a certain vantage point. In that sense, propaganda is also very close to some conceptions of ideology (as discussed in the previous chapter), or the way certain perceptions of the world are privileged over others.

This wisdom has largely disappeared from recent debates on fake news, misinformation, disinformation, alternative facts, and similar conceptual frameworks activated in relation to events such as the armed conflict in Ukraine, the Brexit referendum, Russian interference in the US election in 2016, and the Cambridge Analytica scandal in 2018, among others. Thus, a concept such as "computational propaganda" can be defined as "a communicative practice" that utilizes "algorithms, automation, and human curation to purposefully manage and distribute misleading information over social media networks" (Woolley and Howard 2019, 4). As Johan Farkas and Jannick Schou (2020) have convincingly shown, such simplified discourses about truth (and its opposite) have been prominent in the explosion of both academic and nonacademic literature following these various scandals. An exception that stands out is Peter Pomerantsev's study of contemporary "influence operations" around the world, in which he devotes one chapter to Ukraine-Russia relations. Referring to Ellul, he insists that "one has to look beyond 'news' and 'politics' to understand . . . 'the formation of men's attitude'" (Pomerantsev 2019, 10). Pomerantsev also makes the point that *propaganda* is a term so "fraught and fractured" that he avoids using it. Consequently, his book is titled *This Is Not Propaganda*.

One can debate the analytical usefulness of concepts such as fake news and disinformation on the grounds laid out in early propaganda research (e.g., by Ellul and others), but the circulation of messages needs to be theoretically framed and dealt with. Given today's numerous media formats, messages, stories, and signs circulate among various communication levels and platforms, from interpersonal communication to niche media to mass media. In such complex communication structures, it is worth examining how messages are remediated, assembled, circulated, and made sense of at different moments of communication.

In Hall's (1973) encoding-decoding model, the encoded mass media message is surrounded by contextual factors: frames of knowledge, technological infrastructure, relations of production. Hall constructed these ideas in the early 1970s to study the production of "meaningful discourse" in television, and these three contextual conditions for production were and still are undeniably important. However, in the present landscape, texts as meaningful discourse do not result only from encoding processes in the television studio and, in the context of generic understanding, technological means and organizational principles of production. They also arrive from the circulation of already communicated texts and text fragments in the "semiosphere" (Lotman [1984] 2005), or the realm of circulation of signs (cf. Verón 2014). Contemporary mass media production has a much richer repertoire of prefabricated images to appropriate, in the form of narrative formulas and generic props produced elsewhere, in other media technologies. This "elsewhere" consists of both the continuously growing archive of images and text fragments of earlier mass media productions and the snippets of videos, images, and texts posted by small-scale media "produsers" on social media platforms (Bruns 2006), which are then remediated in other social media and in the mass media.

Textual fragments, images, and signs produced and circulated on the local or regional level are constantly remediated and ultimately picked up by larger media organizations with international reach (Bolter and Grusin 2000). Studying these processes of circulation in their totality is onerous and requires large research teams. Although such approaches have their limits, in that they can focus only on small, circumscribed events, the results can be rewarding. Argentinian media researcher and semiotician Mario Carlón (2020a, 2020b) has developed an analytical model for the circulation of media messages around specific communicative events, whereby he separates various types of mediated communication.

As shown in figure 3.1, Carlón aims to capture how media messages circulate from applications such as WhatsApp, Messenger, and similar interpersonal media; over social media networks such as Facebook, Twitter, and Instagram; to the mass media of television, radio, and newspapers (online

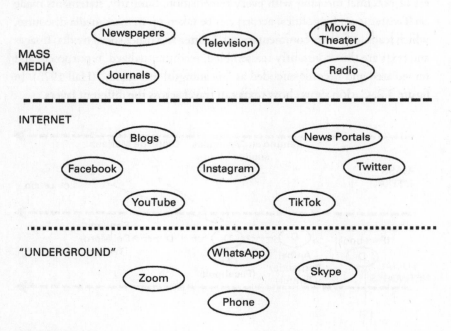

Figure 3.1
Principles of circulation.
Figure by Mario Carlón (2020a, 229)

or offline). Circulation occurs not only from niche media to mass media; it often happens in the opposite direction. In fact, much of what is distributed on niche media is not generated by users. Media scholar Lothar Mikos (2010) has argued that rather than "user-generated content," a better term would be "user-distributed content," since much of what circulates on Facebook, Twitter, and YouTube is actually produced by the traditional media industries and then relayed by social media users. These users are working as veritable "slave-transmitters," having become part of the marketing and promotion activities of traditional mass media productions within entertainment and reality shows.

These various types of media technologies, and their affordances when it comes to circulating images and texts, can be thought of as different layers in the communications universe. With the help of such a model, one can empirically study how messages circulate between these different layers. For example, images from the mass media become memes on social media networks and can then resurface in the mass media in a dialogic fashion that adds new layers of potential meaning with every remediation. Similarly, statements made on Twitter (e.g., by political actors) can be taken up in mass media discourse, which leads to further commentary on Twitter and other social media. Images and texts are thus constantly reassembled, recontextualized, repurposed, and remediated and become encoded as "meaningful discourses" (Hall 1973). In figure 3.2, Carlón shows how texts can travel across the different layers.

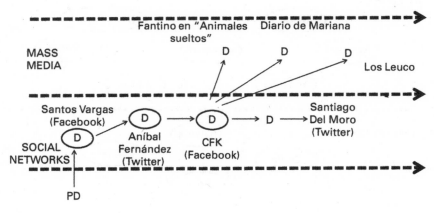

Figure 3.2
Example of circulation.
Figure by Mario Carlón (2020a, 231)

A full-blown study of the circulation of texts around the Euromaidan events would be possible in principle, but it is beyond the scope of this inquiry. However, we use the ideas of circulation and remediation to analyze how different media technologies are adopted and used before stories are formed in the mass media and eventually reappear in niche and networking media. The analysis starts with the Facebook call for action on the Maidan; next, Hromadske TV, Espreso TV, Spilno.tv, UkrStream.tv, Radio Svoboda, and other online broadcasters produced images for web platforms such as YouTube; these were later picked up by the mass media in various countries, as well as by international broadcasters such as CNN and BBC World (see Szostek 2014, 7ff.).

CIRCULATION OF NEWS IMAGES OF THE
EUROMAIDAN REVOLUTION

The established narrative about the Revolution of Dignity on Euromaidan is that it started on 21 November 2013 when President Viktor Yanukovych surprisingly refused to sign the association agreement between Ukraine and the European Union and journalist Mustafa Nayem sent out a call on Facebook for people to rally on Independence Square (Maidan Nezalezhnosti) the same evening (see, e.g., Junes 2016; Dyczok 2014). As Olga Onuch (2015a, 171) has shown, Nayem was not the only one summoning people to Maidan, but because he was already a well-known journalist, his Facebook post has been highlighted for the history books.[1] At the time, Nayem was working at the newly established Hromadske TV; the channel had been founded in June but had not yet started broadcasting. However, it went on the air on 22 November when protesters began gathering in large numbers at the square, and it continued around-the-clock reporting during the turbulent events. In addition to Hromadske, Espreso TV and UkrStream broadcast continuously from strategically placed positions around the Maidan. These live streams quickly became important sources for other international and national media organizations such as CNN, BBC, and SVT. Several other media platforms and organizations were born during the Maidan events, most of which distributed news through social media such as VKontakte, Facebook, or Twitter. Many of these platforms were thus part of the revolution, forming the activists' media and information wing. Press and media centers in various forms were clearly an important part of the Euromaidan

Revolution, and like Hromadske, some of them are still active, such as Euromaidan Press.

In the images of events that took place on Maidan Nezalezhnosti in late 2013 and early 2014, media technologies are rarely visible. Most commonly, these images show crowds of people participating in protests on the square, piles of tires, or scenes of violence. However, the media presence is apparent because the whole long event took place in front of cameras that were broadcasting live. Events were continually reported in short tweets and even longer commentaries and analyses on Facebook and VKontakte. In effect, this was a mediated revolution, or even a mediatized revolution, in the sense that it evolved along with the media. This specific type of "live broadcasting of history," as Daniel Dayan and Elihu Katz (1992) famously explain, adds a new dimension to the immediacy produced by liveness, the feeling that one is taking part in historical events as they happen. The difference between the mediatized Euromaidan events and Dayan and Katz's live broadcasting of history is that those events were preplanned outside of the media institutions; those institutions then magnified the events and added a specific kind of ceremonial reverence to them. In the case of the Euromaidan Revolution, there was no preplanning that would have given the large international media institutions enough time to orchestrate the event on every channel. In this specific case, the mediatization of the event occurred not through the mass media but through *other* media: the social media of Twitter, Facebook, and VKontakte, but also the live streams by Hromadske TV, Espreso TV, and other online media services. One could say that the Euromaidan events were mediated before they were narrated.

A major point of Dayan and Katz's media events theory is that the media event is a specific "narrative genre" in its own right—a genre that follows specific narrative tropes of "contests," "conquests," and "coronations." The Euromaidan events might be said to fit into a subset of these tropes that Dayan and Katz call *transformative* (1992, 167ff.). The narrative structure presupposes clear roles in such events—protagonists and antagonists, heroes and villains. And there are sequential steps in the narrative.

Most accounts of the role of the media during the Euromaidan Revolution focus on the organizational aspects of the protests (see, e.g., Metzger and Tucker 2017; Onuch 2015b) and the ways social media and interpersonal communication technologies (ICTs) such as text messages and messenger services connected the active protesters and updated them about the events:

"ICTs allowed activists to facilitate connectivity, coordinate the mobilization process, speed up the flow of information, and create opportunities for grassroots self-organization by 'ordinary' citizens who participated in the protests" (Onuch 2015a, 170).

As Ukrainian Canadian historian Marta Dyczok (2016, 7) reports, very few Western mass media organizations had correspondents in Ukraine during the initial phases of the Euromaidan events. Smaller media outlets such as EuromaidanPR (not to be confused with Euromaidan Press) published continual updates, and images from the various live streaming platforms such as Hromadske TV were picked up by international mass media for wider dissemination to international audiences (Metzger and Tucker 2017). In addition, both short and long stories and analyses of the ongoing situation were published on social media in English. Images also spread quite rapidly this way, being picked up by international media and by interested social media users abroad. Several local journalists and PR professionals were among the protesters, and they had access to international networks that could spread stories from the Maidan. Later, these networks were useful in disseminating information from other sites of conflict, such as Crimea, as well as news about Malaysian airliner MH37, which was shot down over eastern Ukraine (see Onuch 2015a).

This is nothing new. Amateur and nonprofessional footage has always seeped into the mainstream mass media. Photography was arguably the first amateur medium to enter into news reporting, and when portable and relatively cheap video cameras arrived, this led to an increase in the use of amateur footage. Famous examples include the beating of Rodney King by police in Los Angeles in the early 1990s (Fiske 1994, 125ff.) and, more recently, the killing of George Floyd by police in Minneapolis (see, e.g., Ciechalski, Fichtel, and Abdelkader 2020). With the explosion of social media in the early twenty-first century, the sheer amount of recorded material in the form of photos and videos changed news reporting forever. And, of course, the Euromaidan events are no exception. What makes Euromaidan a bit different from similar newsworthy events is that few representatives of international media were present during the initial stages of the upheaval, which made amateur and small media broadcasters' footage essential.

Another difference between Euromaidan and the live broadcasts of history that Dayan and Katz (1992) focus on—the moon landing, Anwar Sadat's visit to Israel, the Olympic Games—is that their examples are from a less cluttered

media landscape. In the age of broadcast television, large national broadcasters could dominate the media flows and cut through all channels. As the
dominant medium, television also set the agenda for news reporting in the
press and on radio. The situation today is different. First, the multiplication
of television channels has been dramatic, if not exponential. This is especially true in Europe, where, up until the late 1980s, television was heavily
dominated by public service companies (see Ellis 2000)—often modeled on
the ideal of the BBC—or state television, which was the dominant form in
the Soviet Union and eastern Europe (see Mihelj and Huxtable 2018). In the
"era of plenty," as Ellis calls it, there is an abundance of television channels ranging from regional to national to transnational. Second, television
does not occupy the dominant position it enjoyed fifty years ago. Online
media have radically changed the landscape, giving birth to multiple media
forms, including social media, blogs, and various smartphone applications.
These formats have become part of people's media ensembles—leading to
the increased circulation of signs, messages, and information today.

Euromaidan events boosted the use of social media in Ukraine substantially. At the time, the most popular social networking platforms were the
Russian-based VKontakte and OdnoKlasniki, with 27 million and 11 million
users, respectively. Facebook was also popular, with a little more than 3 million users (Onuch 2015a, 174). Twitter had relatively few users in Ukraine
before Euromaidan, but numbers doubled between July 2013 and July 2014.
The growth in Twitter use took off in the beginning of December, coincid-
ing with the escalation in protests and violence. The most popular hashtag
during this time was the Ukrainian-language version of *Euromaidan* (Metzger
and Tucker 2017, 177).

Although Facebook and Twitter had much smaller user bases than VKontakte and OdnoKlasniki, Facebook, Twitter, and VKontakte became the
Euromaidan protesters' preferred communication tools. Unsurprisingly,
Twitter fulfilled different functions than the other two, being used mainly for
organizational purposes among journalists and protesters—two groups that
were sometimes hard to separate (Onuch 2015a, 175). Facebook and VKontakte were more popular among "ordinary" protesters. Whereas social media
were important for the protesters in Kyiv and for international audiences, live-
streamed reports were important sources of information for audiences outside
of Kyiv and for raising support for the protesters (Onuch 2015a, 177ff.).

The fact that images circulate among the different types of media means
that there are mismatches between how participants perceive events and how

they are represented in the mass media. One example concerns the focus on the radical right-wing group Pravyi Sektor (Right Sector), which "until mid-December [was] simply a location in the Maidan protest zone . . . in the right-hand corner of the Square" (Onuch 2015b, 37). The homology between the group's physical position on the square and its political orientation seemingly amplified its importance when images circulated in the international media. BBC News (2014) reported that Pravyi Sektor "played a leading role" in clashes with the police in January.

Nick Couldry (2000) has analyzed the relations between people's first-hand knowledge and experiences of protest events and "the media frame," or how these same events are reported in the media. This analysis is relevant to the circulation of narratives around Euromaidan and the events following in its wake. Couldry found that people who had firsthand knowledge of events did not think the reporting was accurate and thus "had their trust in the media disrupted" (2000, 180). Couldry juxtaposed the protesters' stories with how they were reported in the media, with a focus on how the media images then became "denaturalised." In contrast, the circulation of images from Ukraine illustrates the discrepancies between images and narratives on social media and the wider reporting of those events in international mass media. The mass media stories are thus weighed not only against firsthand experiences of events but also against how the images and texts circulate in social and niche media, which may be a combination of firsthand experience and social media perceptions. It is not always possible to uphold a distinction between the mediation of an event and the event itself. Social and niche media thus add to the repertoire of technologies that inform how signs, words, and narratives circulate, and they have an impact on the circulating texts as meaningful discourse.

An example of this discrepancy is the role of the right-wing protesters in Pravyi Sektor and Svoboda at Maidan. Many have cited their minor role in the protests (e.g., Likhachev 2014; Umland and Shekhovtsov 2014). Volodomyr Ishchenko (2016), who performed a systematic review of data from the protests, found that the media reported on both groups to a disproportionate degree, especially in relation to violent or confrontational events, so he therefore concluded that they were actually important during the protests. However, the fact that a group is overrepresented does not mean that it is important. Rather, such a group's prominence can be seen in the light of the journalistic logic that privileges confrontation over peaceful protests. In the long run, biased reporting can indeed become part of a narrative about an event such as Euromaidan, and it can be used for various purposes in the form of latently strategic and systematically distorted communication (Habermas [1976] 1979). Such types of communication need not always be in narrative format with narrative closure; they can just as easily circulate as propositional discourses—snippets of information strategically doled out in various media platforms and outlets to destabilize or provoke uncertainty.

The connections between social, niche, and mass media exemplify one type of circulation that ultimately results in an overarching narrative or at least a meaningful discourse. There are, however, other forms of circulation, related to other media technologies, with a less pronounced narrative form. In the next section, we examine the circulation of signs within the PR sector prior to the Euromaidan events. Their morphology is of the utmost importance for understanding meaning management during and after the revolution as well.

THE CIRCULATION OF NATIONALIST SYMBOLS VIA POWERPOINT

More than the representation of events is involved in the circulation of signs. These signs are circulated diachronically as well as synchronously between narratives and stories. For example, as noted in the previous chapter, the fact that the TV channel Ukraine Today (UT) chose "to inform, unite, and influence" as its motto is significant, considering the dramatic changes in the media landscape over the nearly one hundred years since John Reith (1924) coined the BBC's similar slogan "to inform, educate, and entertain." No doubt, the BBC also worked to unite the British Empire—after all, the BBC Empire Service was launched in 1932 for this specific purpose (Potter 2012)—but Reith and his contemporaries presumably would not agree to equate the public value of education to the more manipulative and instrumental concept of influence (although Ellul [1965] might). The general idea behind UT's motto is to build on similarity, in the hope that the goodwill enjoyed by the BBC will spill over to its Ukrainian counterpart. Such spillover effects are often sought in PR and advertising, and in nation branding campaigns, the nation's images and symbols circulate among different media formats, remediated from print to visuals, taking advantage of historical as well as contemporary visual tropes. Such remediating practices have been taken advantage of by some of the agents discussed in the previous chapter, and here we rewind the tape to a time preceding the tumultuous events on

Maidan Nezalezhnosti to see how images were circulated in the various media involved in nation branding campaigns.

Branding is a practice whereby the creative agents, those who manage and encode the actual messages into meaningful discourse, must produce their own market. Most often, this involves presenting an idea to those who might pay for its further development. Take, for example, CFC's efforts to convince the Ukrainian government to launch the "Ukraine Inspires" campaign in 2010. This prospective campaign, directed toward foreign investors, painted a picture of Ukraine as an attractive post-Soviet country where one could make profitable investments. The brand book CFC produced had a spectacular glossy design and a twenty- by eighty-centimeter format—not exactly something visitors at a business fair or exhibition center would pick up and put in their briefcases to take home. Instead, it was meant for an audience of state administrators and politicians to display on their desktops, with the aim of convincing this exclusive audience to put up money for the campaign.

Branding campaigns typically adopt the media of public relations and advertising, such as billboards, commercials, and event marketing, but also "native content" in specialized media such as in-flight magazines, tourist brochures, and the like (Bolin and Ståhlberg 2010). More importantly, in the initial phases of a nation branding campaign, at the moment national images are constructed, other kinds of media are adopted, including a brand book (as described above) and presentational software or "slideware" (Schoenborn 2013), such as PowerPoint, Keynote, and Prezi. In this context, we are interested in how slideware is used to circulate national images at the initiation of a nation branding campaign. Arguably, the specific character of presentation tools and how they are used in the early stages of a nation branding campaign also have an impact in later stages. Presentation tools have received little research attention, which might seem strange, given that they have become widespread since the launch of PowerPoint in 1977 (Kernbach, Bresciani, and Eppler 2015, 293). Slideware is unbiquitous in diverse settings such as education, corporate business, academic research, and urban planning (Tufte 2003; Yates and Orlikowski 2007; Knoblauch 2008; Stark and Paravel 2008), and it has affected the work practices in many of these fields, converging with postindustrial modes of production. Much of the research into PowerPoint practice has focused on the cognitive, emotional, and social constraints of the medium (Kernbach, Bresciani, and Eppler 2015), although some have also considered its affordances (Stark and Paravel 2008).

In addition to being a rhetorical instrument (Kjeldsen 2006), PowerPoint is a structuring technology with it own specific morphology (Stark and Paravel 2008). In many instances, PowerPoint is masked as a presentation, yet it is the actual result of the work carried out in marketing divisions and organizational administration. In the past, the marketing department would deliver a written report to the corporate board and then make a presentation with the aid of slideware. Today, there is no report, and the board is presented with a printed deck of slides (Yates and Orlikowski 2007), something we discuss at length elsewhere (Bolin and Ståhlberg 2021). These slide shows take on a life of their own as they are circulated on corporate webpages or on special platforms such as SlideShare and then distributed on social networking sites such as LinkedIn and Facebook, forming a repository of images and bullet points that can be reused and remediated endlessly in new combinations.

Several researchers have argued that a PowerPoint presentation does not constitute a complete whole; it cannot stand by itself and has to be understood contextually to a much larger extent than most other media genres. Scholars disagree about what that context should be. For Hubert Knoblauch (2008), it is the live presentation, in which the technology interacts with an audience and a presenter. JoAnne Yates and Wanda Orlikowski (2007) regard the organization in which the PowerPoint presentation is produced as the contextual unit of analysis. Dennis Schoenborn (2013) discusses context in terms of genre, while David Stark and Verena Paravel (2008) adopt a larger perspective and focus on political issues germane to a certain public as the relevant context. For slideware used in nation branding, the context can be extended even further because each stack of slides is linked not only to the immediate local context of involved producers and other actors but also to previous campaigns and even the whole international field of branding as such. Outside any context of promotional culture and practice, a PowerPoint presentation on nation branding would be fundamentally incomprehensible. Thus, PowerPoint does not lend itself to the construction of narratives in isolation from other media and apart from the context of presentation. There is no stable structure, no unquestionable beginning or end, no plot or coherent story in a stack of presentation slides. As a media form, a PowerPoint presentation lacks integrity; its texts and images invite restructuring. This is perhaps the role of PowerPoint: to provide building blocks that can be assembled to create narrative wholes.

POWERPOINTING UKRAINE

In the spring of 2013 the Ukrainian Tourism Authorities initiated a new campaign intended to attract more tourists to the country. The previous year Ukraine, together with Poland, had hosted the European Football Championship, Euro 2012, so it had some recent experience in attracting foreign attention. The various PR campaigns that year had suffered from domestic criticism, causing those responsible to withdraw (Ståhlberg and Bolin 2016). The bid for a new tourist brand concept was won by a small and loosely organized company called WikiCityNomica (WCN).

WCN's company structure is much more informal than that of most established international PR companies, yet it shares this structural fluidity with other small PR companies in Ukraine (and possibly elsewhere). One might say that its company structure is homologous with slideware technology as a medium. WCN does not have a permanent office; nor does it have employees with clear-cut designations. Rather, it is a network of people loosely structured around a few individuals; they present themselves as a creative team in some contexts and as a think tank in others. Often, they seem to regard themselves as a voluntary organization of idealists, working for a just cause rather than for profit.

WCN presented the initial results of its work at the Second Kyiv International Tourism Forum on 10 October 2013. This large and important event was opened by the vice prime minister of Ukraine, Oleksandr Vilkul, and visited by several other domestic and foreign dignitaries.[2] Vilkul announced the strategy of the campaign, which, among other things, included destination branding of world heritage sites and of the jewel in the crown of the Ukrainian tourism industry: Crimea. The ambitious aim was to double the annual inflow of tourists from 25 million in 2013 to 50 million in 2022. Much of the hope for this future growth was tied to the upcoming association agreement with the European Union free-trade market, to be signed in November. "Tourism," Vilkul said in his opening speech, "is a diplomatic asset now" (figure 3.3).

The presentation of the new tourism brand concept was scheduled for the following day. In addition to meetings between ministers and exhibitions from various countries and regions, it included the showcasing of major upcoming or planned international events taking place in Ukraine, such as EuroBasket 2015 and the Winter Olympic Games in 2022.[3]

Figure 3.3
Expected tourist inflow to Ukraine.
Source: PowerPoint slide presented at the Second Kyiv International Forum,
downloaded from Oleksandr Vilkul's Facebook page, 10 October 2013, https://www
.facebook.com/475147705910715/photos/pb.100044526215703.-2207520000
../543188399106645/?type=3

The press conference at which WCN introduced itself and its initial
efforts was a rather modest event, taking place in a seminar room rather
than one of the main exhibition halls. Hosting the presentation was Valerii
Pekar, representing WCN. It was evident that the new Ukraine brand was
still a work in progress. There were several presentations by partners WCN
had worked with previously, such as municipal authorities from Kharkiv,
Donetsk, Lviv, and Odesa, who recounted recent efforts to rebrand their
cities. Importantly, the focus of the event was on the significance of place
branding in general, rather than on the new Ukrainian concept in particular.
Needless to say, all the presentations were accompanied by PowerPoint slides.

In his presentation, Pekar explained that the new national brand would
be built on the traditional Ukrainian reluctance to choose between alternatives: it would be "and-and" rather than "either-or." That allowed the
creation of a "myth" of Ukraine as a place of integration, innovation, and

transformation—a myth that foreign tourists would appreciate. In the PowerPoint slides he demonstrated how logos, slogans, music, and commercials would be built on this idea of "and-and."

These ideas never materialized. The campaign was halted only a couple of months later when demonstrations and violence hit the streets of Kyiv, including the Ukrainian house where the conference had been held. When the violence escalated and people were killed in front of international news audiences, the idea of attracting tourists became impossible. Thus, just a few weeks after WCN started working on the design and outline of the campaign material, the project was interrupted and, seemingly, a lot of time and effort were wasted—but not completely. WCN continued, without government funding, to present parts of the concept in other contexts and at various conferences within the spheres of both voluntary civil society and commercial business. As early as spring 2014, the brand concept was used in a small project commissioned by companies trying to promote the city of Kyiv, rather than Ukraine at large, as a tourist destination. WCN had been involved with city branding since 2010. Its competence consisted in arranging meetings and presenting ideas to convince stakeholders to cooperate, and it was based on this experience that WCN had competed for and won the tender to design a new brand Ukraine concept.

The working procedures of WCN and its partners were heavily centered on PowerPoint. In fact, on an internet search for WCN, the first six hits were not to its defunct website or to its Facebook page but to SlideShare (slideshare .net) and DocShare (documents.tips), where some of its PowerPoint presentations can be found. These PowerPoint presentations represent different stages in WCN's work as well as different target audiences. In addition, live presentations can be viewed on the company's Facebook page. Table 3.1 lists four decks of slides created for Ukraine, all versions that were available on the internet at some point (in both English and Ukrainian).

Table 3.1
Four PowerPoint slide decks for the Ukrainian tourist brand

Slide compilation	Number of slides
Ukraine's tourist brand (the concept)	42
Ukraine tourism brand: concept, graphic, strategic ideas	70
Ukraine: mission and cultural codes	27
Guiding principles of Ukrainian tourism brand	109

The version titled "Ukraine's tourist brand (the concept)" was presented at the tourist forum in October 2013—a deck of forty-two slides. The slides juxtapose opposites such as Catholicism and Orthodoxy, Christianity and Islam, Europe and Asia, East and West, Ukraine as a "joining edge" that insists on a "denial of choice." Despite emphasizing this intermediate position, the messages are addressed to "people of the Western world, sick of high speeds and self-determination" (slide 22). At the forum, Pekar's colleague at WCN, Tatiana Zhdanova, elaborated on this symbolic duality, arguing that the brand image represents two polarities or alternatives that are usually opposed but in the Ukrainian context coexist. This was also the aim in the graphic design of the icons and the letter *U*.

In a way, the collection is typical of this kind of presentation: a sequence of slides building up an argument through bullet points and images. The presentational form is "show-and-tell," where the image illustrates the words on the screen (Tufte 2003). Thus, the caption "Catholicity and Orthodoxy" is illustrated by an embrace between two priests (figure 3.4). Pekar explained

Catholicity and Orthodoxy

Figure 3.4
Illustration of the concept of the Ukrainian tourist brand.
Source: Valerii Pekar, "Ukraine's Tourist Brand (The Concept)" (presentation, Second Kyiv International Tourism Forum, Kyiv, Ukraine, 10 October 2013).

that the concept had been tried out in workshops across the country: eighty workshops conducted over forty days.

Two of the other slideware collections are similar to the version presented at the Tourist Forum. The one titled "Ukraine tourism brand: concept, graphic, strategic ideas" (in Ukrainian) consists of seventy slides and is an expanded version of the ideas presented in the previously described slide show. The main difference is that the visual concept is given more space.

The other collection, "Ukraine: mission and cultural codes," is a shorter version (twenty-seven slides) of "Ukraine tourism brand." It consists mainly of images, many of them found in the other collections as well. It is explicitly constructed to receive feedback from the audience and was the one used in the workshops mentioned earlier. It was obviously produced to accompany the larger collection of seventy slides and prompts the audience at both the beginning and the end:

> Your feedback is very important to make the brand more visible and attractive.
>
> We kindly invite you to share with us your thoughts, associations, emotions, when you see this. Is the graphic system original, nice, memorable? Do you like it? Does it represent Ukraine, in your opinion? Do you recommend any changes or additions?

The three first collections are not dated, and it is not immediately obvious in which order they were produced. The fourth deck of slides, "Guiding principles of Ukrainian tourism brand," is dated January 2014—at which time the campaign had been interrupted. Thus, this is the final result of the campaign's design stage: the brand book. The brand book was also produced in the slideware medium and uses many of the images and bullet points featured in the other three versions. However, it has more elaborate textual sections and is structured like a report, with a contents page (figure 3.5).

The brand book consists of 109 slides (or pages). The introduction describes it as a resource for "travel industry and hospitality professionals," identified as those who work with "tourism, hotels and restaurants, entertainment, culture, sports, business centres and event organizers, passenger traffic, etc." (slide 3). This is clearly the end product of the first stage of the nation branding campaign. Its target audience is not those who have financed or contributed to WCN's work up to this point; nor is it directed to a general audience—international or domestic. It is directed to those who will be executing the public branding campaign: "travel industry and hospitality professionals." The introduction to the brand book is signed by the

Brand-Platform

System of Visual Identity

Figure 3.5
Content pages of the brand book.
Source: Valerii Pekar, "Guiding Principles of Ukrainian Tourism Brand," January 2014

National Agency for Tourism and Resorts, which funded the work that preceded the book's production (and to which the previous slide collections were primarily addressed). The receiver of earlier messages has now taken on the role of sender.

The brand book is divided into two parts. The first "analytical" part describes the research and development processes behind the end result, its expected outcomes, and the values on which the brand is built. The second, larger part of the brand book (slides 26–109), "System of Visual Identity of Ukrainian Tourist Brand," displays and explains the logotypes, photos, color scheme, fonts (Oksana Cyrillic heavy and Kolyada regular for headings, OfficinaSans C and Tahoma regular for body text), gesture, jingle, animation, and so forth. The combination of these items is supposed to create a discursive universe or myth, "a special world with its own rules and characters" (slide 20). Such discursive universes are generally situated within the frameworks of specific genres—in this case, a commercially laden generic national universe—much as other nation-states construct their mythical realms. However, the slides in this presentation are not intended to build such a myth. The message is that the addressees, the executers of future branding campaigns, should construct the mythical narratives of Ukraine. The brand book offers only guidelines and a repository of images that can be reassembled for that purpose.

The Euromaidan events effectively brought Ukraine's nation branding efforts to a standstill in January 2014. However, the inherent potential of reconfiguration became useful for organizations and individuals engaged in the country's meaning management. The fluid nature of presentational media is homologous with the fluid nature of how the branding and PR business works in Kyiv. Just as the PowerPoint slides can be reshuffled to best fit the context at hand, people move seamlessly between different professional identities, as illustrated by the business cards they hand out. Both companies and people present themselves variably as PR professionals, consultants, NGOs, members of think tanks, and so on. It is illustrative that the leader behind WCN soon cofounded a new civic platform—The New Country—for reforming Ukraine. Thus, he brought his skills in meaning management from the branding context to the post-Maidan situation. And although the speed at which this leading figure moves between companies and professional identities is somewhat extraordinary, the pattern of action is not unique. One could say that people and PowerPoint slides circulate within their respective spheres with the same ease.

CONCLUSION: ASSEMBLAGES OF MEANING

In an opinion piece in the technology magazine *Wired* in 1993, Michael Crichton, author of the best-selling science fiction novel *Jurassic Park*, predicted the mass extinction of the traditional mass media, which were not keeping up with the times and proceeding as if the digital revolution had not happened. US mass media, and especially traditional news media, he argued, had not adapted to the new business models required for the digital age. No doubt journalism and the news media were in deep financial trouble, but it is also clear that the announcement of the death of the mass media was premature. Today, mass, niche, and personal media exist side by side and in symbiotic relationships with one another, not least in the area of news reporting and information dissemination, where messages, information, text, and images circulate almost frictionlessly between them. But other technologies have also entered the general media landscape. Presentational technologies such as PowerPoint have become integrated into the contemporary media milieu in workplaces and in professional life, just as personal and niche media have become part of the everyday lives of citizens in Ukraine and elsewhere. In this milieu, communication technologies contribute to the circulation and reassembling of fragments of meaning in a way that produces a constant flux, rather than the construction of a stable, meaningful whole. Social and niche media have become integrated in the universe in which news images, texts, and fragments circulate. Contemporary media technologies are not characterized by the unified, stable narratives of the old, traditional mass media (e.g., novel, newspaper, film, broadcast television), with their professional production processes strictly separated from the audience. During the Euromaidan events, this was accentuated because the interplay between social networking media and online broadcasting services played such a crucial role. The events took place within a nonnarrative media environment. Texts, signs, and images about the events circulated openly and in abundance, available for a multiplicity of agents to appropriate and use for different purposes.

In the next chapter we look at some of the key events of meaning management during and after the Euromaidan Revolution. Rather than coherent stories reported through traditional news media, we focus on disparate fragments of meaning circulating through a variety of technologies and media forms. Not least, we take note of media management launched outside both mass media and social networking media. Some of the more provocative communication projects have taken the form of physical objects, installations, or designs configured to be circulated and remediated by multiple media technologies. These communication initiatives rely on a conviction that a clear-cut message or coherent story is not needed because other actors with other technologies will continue to build assemblages of meaning.

MEDIA EVENTS AND MEANING MANAGEMENT

> Before this message can have an "effect" (however defined), or satisfy a "need"
> or be put to a "use," it must first be perceived as a meaningful discourse and
> meaningfully decoded.
> —Stuart Hall (1973, 3)

Since the winter of 2013–2014 and the dramatic and intense discursive struggles around the Euromaidan, several crucial events have occurred, some of
which have been narrativized and shaped into stories and representations of
Ukraine. Since 2013, Ukraine has repeatedly appeared on the international
news agenda, and the country has certainly been "put on the map," but
perhaps in unpredictable ways and always at the will of a wide variety of
agents and through a range of media technologies and forms. This chapter
looks more closely at the actual texts, messages, and *narratives* produced by
the agents presented in chapter 2 and circulated via the technologies and
media forms discussed in chapter 3. We discuss the content and information
managed in relation to two media events taking place between 2014 and
2017. First, we examine how the Euromaidan events themselves became
narrated and, in particular, how they became narrated as a *media event*. We
follow Daniel Dayan and Elihu Katz's (1992) model for how such events
are narrated, with a specific focus on their transformative aspects. Second,
we discuss the different types of information and meaning management
conducted in preparation for the Eurovision Song Contest (ESC) in Kyiv
in May 2017. As in previous chapters, this discussion builds on interviews
with mass media representatives, PR consultants, political administrators,
and brand designers, plus an analysis of branding materials, including the
design of logotypes and other representations.

THE NARRATIVE ORDER OF TRANSFORMATIVE MEDIA EVENTS

We have argued throughout this book that managing information is a type of strategic communication practice that ultimately aims to produce meaning—to arrange things, people, and events in a way that makes them meaningful for oneself as well as for others. This idea goes back to Enlightenment philosophy and is, for example, the basis of Immanuel Kant's thinking: the world is an assemblage of myriad things, places, events, happenings, signs, and people, all framed in historical circumstance (which, of course, must also be constructed in order to appear intelligible). Our faculties are not reliable, so we seek meaning by making things coherent to us, giving them a purpose, a reason for their existence and for our knowledge of them. Thus, we construct narratives that are meaningful.

To construct narratives and make them interpretable to others is, as Jürgen Habermas ([1981] 1992) eloquently elaborates in his *Theory of Communicative Action*, a form of social action. Habermas distinguishes between two types of social action: *communicative action*, aimed at achieving consensus and understanding, and *strategic action*, which is goal oriented, instrumental, and aimed at exerting influence either openly (e.g., advertising) or covertly (i.e., "latently strategic"). This latter type of action is manipulative, masking its own intentions; it can also be systematically distortive and misleading (e.g., lies). This type of strategic communication can, of course, be disguised to appear communicative while actually being deceptive. Commercial textual examples of this kind include stealth or native advertising, shills, astroturfing, and advergaming—all of which hide their commercial intention in order to persuade the target audience to buy a product (or a political message). Whether these practices are deceptive or not is an empirical question for reception research. In this chapter we focus on the messages themselves, putting aside questions of their social reception.

Dayan and Katz provide us with some theoretical tools to approach narrative structures in media events. Of specific interest for our analysis is the subset of events they label "transformative"—those events that address a latent conflict or crisis, propose change, and can ultimately lead to real social change. One of their main examples is "the live broadcast of the mass demands for political change in Eastern Europe in 1989" (Dayan and Katz 1992, 147). Such ceremonial transformative media events "address a latent conflict," enact "a reorganization of time and space—that is, of history and geography," and make "formerly unthinkable solutions thinkable" (160).

Dayan and Katz cite mass television broadcasting as the key medium, but in relation to the mass protests in Prague in 1989, they also note the strong presence of what they refer to as "small media": "the 'alternative media' of revolution—graffiti, posters, pamphlets, illegal books and newspapers, church rallies and pilgrimages, agitation at factories, and word-of-mouth on the streets—to mobilize hundreds of thousands of people for the now-nightly rallies" (1992, 157). The small media were especially important in the eastern European protests because the state controlled the mass media at the time. Naturally, these small or alternative media were of a different kind in 1989 than they were in 2013, but it is not hard to see the parallel between graffiti, posters, and pamphlets and contemporary social media and their role as communication tools among protesters.

A transformative media event, Dayan and Katz propose, is a "narrative genre" with its own "typical sequential structure"; the events "follow a recognizable scenario of progress through a succession of identifiable phases" that "echoes the phase theories that anthropologists have applied to change processes such as rites of passage" (1992, 176).[1] More precisely, they argue that the transformative event goes through five phases that can be summarized as follows (167–168):

1. A "longstanding problem" that precedes the event and acts as the condition to which the event is a response.
2. The announcement of a ceremonial event: a "signalling that reawakens silenced aspirations."
3. The start of the event itself, introduced with a "gesture that is presented as an instrumental step toward solving the problem."
4. The enactment of gestures and messages by ceremonial leaders.
5. The aftermath of the event.

The first and the last phases are not really part of the event itself but can be said to frame it. In the first phase, we are presented with a "longstanding problem that is considered crippling and incurable." In this case, the latent problem is the perceived dependence on Russia, compounded by the frustration provoked by a corrupt economic and political system that limits people's opportunities to prosper. The tension related to Russia has a long history dating back several hundred years, but it was reactualized through the collapse of the Soviet Union and Ukraine's fragile independence.

This tension is the condition for the second phase, which begins with the "announcement of an impending ceremonial event" that "reawakens silenced aspirations" and creates "a wave of expectations and public excitement" (Dayan and Katz 1992, 167). In this case, the event is the promised signing of an association agreement with the European Union on 28 November 2013 and the expectation of regaining dignity and national recognition. These expectations were evidenced by Ukraine's desire to be an international player in the tourism business, as clearly articulated at the Kyiv International Tourism Forum in October 2013 (see chapter 3), as well as Ukraine's aspirations to host several European sports events, such as EuroBasket 2015 and the 2022 Winter Olympic Games. But these expectations were also clearly expressed in interviews with representatives of the Ukrainian state, who emphasized the long-standing tensions with Russia and the solution the EU association agreement would provide. As a high official in charge of information policy in the Yanukovych government explained to us in an interview in October 2013:

I guess this government consists of 99% Russian speakers, originating from Eastern part of Ukraine. My boss, Kostyantyn Gryshchenko, is one of the few that speaks Ukrainian, not only at office, but also at home. . . . First and foremost, there was a great process of disillusionment with Russia. A disillusionment in principle . . . for myself as well, I worked for two years in the Ukrainian embassy in Moscow. A disillusionment in the principal opportunity to get fair and equal treatment. We were always treated as second class. . . . As some artificial country. They still think that Ukraine appeared by some mistake. It's a historic aberration, not a natural thing. They think a state is like Sweden or Finland but not Ukraine, it's a part of Russia occupied by some strange people. . . . Ukrainians need to understand that they have to do something different to get respect . . . their children study abroad, investment in Europe. They like the modus vivendi of the European Union, and they want to associate themselves with the West. That's why this government . . . and it really did more than any other, in terms of bringing us closer to the European Union. The majority of the population supports it. . . . European integration is associated with progress, associated with developing the right way. It's a great impetus for self-esteem, self-respect . . . yes, we are becoming closer to the most respected countries in the world. They are inviting us. Yeah, ok, economically it's a long way, but still, like we do want to get there somehow. It doesn't matter it's a very fast approach. Especially for the youth, it cannot be substituted for economic benefits, from economic links with Russia. Today you can feel psychologically that no one is satisfied where we are, or those who feel degraded, like we are moving back to the Soviet Union.

Expressed here is a lack of recognition and respect by Russia, a feeling that Ukrainians are treated as inferior and second class when all they want is fair treatment. The opportunity to move closer to the EU is claimed to be in line with general public opinion.[2] This interview was conducted just a couple of weeks before President Yanukovych unexpectedly refrained from signing the EU association agreement. Our informant clearly thought the Yanukovych government was on a steady course toward closer ties with the EU. The sudden change in policy must thus have come as a surprise, even to people in the governmental administration.

This trope is also expressed in commentaries in journals and magazines. It can be described as frustration but also anxiety about the country's image and the need for Ukraine to develop a "success story" (Stolyarchuk 2013).[3] This perception was widespread in the pre-Euromaidan days of early 2013 and is illustrated by several articles in a special May issue of *Kyiv Weekly* titled "Ukraine: Choosing a Face." It is illustrated with a photo of a man in suit and tie holding his faceless, egg-shaped head in his hands, and the articles in the special issue clearly express a longing for recognition. Ukraine was supposedly an anonymous country in the eyes of the world, similar to the widespread image of Ukraine as a "poor, divided and corrupt country with easily accessible women" (Bezpiatchuk 2011).

The aspirations triggered in the second phase were expressed broadly in the mass media, pointing to the act that would bring respect and legitimacy to Ukraine and open up new opportunities, especially for young people. These hopes and aspirations were broken by Yanukovych's refusal to sign the EU agreement. This was followed by what could be called the "media event proper," the event that cut through channels and became a dominant news item in the international media: the protests on Maidan Nezalezhnosti and the subsequent violence and clashes between protesters and police. These protests were a response to the government's broken promises, but they also expressed people's hopes and aspirations relative to "the modus vivendi of the European Union." The protests and violence were quickly covered by social media (Facebook, Twitter, VKontakte) and streamed on "small media" such as Hromadske TV, Spilno TV, and Espreso TV, in addition to online outlets such as Euromaidan Press. They were then relayed to the international news media.

The third phase, following Dayan and Katz's theory, consists of the beginning of the event "in the form of a gesture that is presented as an instrumental step towards solving the problem," with "a modelling or an illustrating of the desirable state of affairs" (Dayan and Katz 1992, 168). This is when the visual medium of television enters into the narrative sequence (Hromadske TV, Espreso TV, CNN, BBC World, and so forth). In relation to the Czechoslovakian uprising, Dayan and Katz point to the fact that state television suddenly started to report on the protests (1992, 175). Similarly— and surprisingly—the main Ukrainian television stations reported on the Euromaidan events in quite neutral terms, despite their social and economic alliances to the president and the loyalties suggested by those bonds.

In the Ukrainian case, the third phase was not as straightforward as Dayan and Katz prescribe. Here, the gesture—signing the EU association agreement—was interrupted by Yanukovych's refusal to sign the agreement. This refusal disrupted the transformative media event and introduced what could be considered a renewed gesture, inspiring action by citizens who desired a closer connection to the European Union. The hopes and aspirations were the same, but the gesture was different, and it was executed by different agents.[4]

The narrativization of the third phase of the event took many forms: uncaptioned images from online broadcasters, snippets of text on social media, and longer written commentaries. A daily ritual soon developed, based on speeches from the Euromaidan stage, interspersed each hour with the singing of the Ukrainian national anthem "Shche ne vmerla Ukraina" (Ukraine has not yet perished), often led by the singer Ruslana, one of the main protagonists. Ukraine's anthem was officially adopted in 1992, after independence, but it dates back to the nationalist movements of the mid-nineteenth century, with music by Mykhailo Verbytsky and lyrics by Ukrainian poet Pavlo Chubynsky. Like many national anthems, Ukraine's has a nationalist theme and is suitable for mass singing. The last line is roughly translated as "We shall be masters in our own home."[5] Another part of the narrative was the repeated overviews of the massive crowd at the Maidan, including agitating speeches from the stage that often ended with the exclamation *Slava Ukraini*—glory to Ukraine.[6]

But there were other recurring features as well. In the early days of the protests, a piano was brought in and became a subplot in the narrative of Euromaidan, heavily documented by various broadcast media as well as on social media.[7] The piano was painted yellow and blue—Ukraine's colors—and moved from place to place on or near the Maidan, including on a burnt-out Berkut bus in front of a long row of police equipped with shields and riot gear. It was played by a man in a black ski mask and combat clothes who called himself "The Piano Extremist," an ironic commentary on the labels given to the protesters by interior minister Vitali Zakharchenko (Novick 2014). He received a fair amount of attention not only from social media but also from mainstream media such as the BBC.[8] Lithuanian filmmaker Vita Maria Drygas also made a TV documentary about the man and his playing called *Piano* (2015).[9] The contrast between the lyrical classical pieces being played on the piano and the rubble on the streets was too tempting not to cover, but it also turned into a sign representing the "human" protesters and the Robocop-like police with their riot gear. The piano's significance in the narrative of the events is confirmed by its inclusion in the 2016 exhibition of Ukrainian revolutions at the National Museum of the History of Ukraine (figure 4.1).

Figure 4.1
The piano at the National Museum of the History of Ukraine. The piano is still there at the time of this writing and can be seen on the museum's virtual tour: https://museum-portal.com/en/museum/national-museum-of-history-of-ukraine/.
Photo by authors, 2016

Another symbolic layer relates to the fact that the piano's brand is "Ukraine," which was the most popular piano brand during the Soviet era.[10]

The disruptive event, which initially lacked the ceremonial dimensions that Dayan and Katz argue are significant markers of transformative media events, gradually aligned with the sequential ordering of the transformative event. First, however, the violence escalated in January 2014, resulting in the killing of many protesters—the so-called Heavenly Hundred, whose portraits were lined up on the side of the Maidan.

Eventually, the disruptive event took on other ritualistic and ceremonial features, such as the repeated singing of the national anthem. Dariya Orlova quotes a Ukrainian classical music composer who said in an interview that the protesters' singing "gained liturgical meaning" that was starkly different from the singing of the anthem at football matches, for example (2016, 221). With the ousting of President Yanukovych, the disruptive event slowly merged and integrated into Dayan and Katz's fourth phase, where "ceremonial performers not only enact gestures, they also deliver straightforward messages" (1992, 168). These messages included speeches from the Euromaidan stage and the singing of the national anthem. In this phase, "utopia is modelled," and "the feasibility of the proposed transformation" is articulated (180). A guest leader is proposed, and in the Euromaidan case, there were several: former elite boxer and member of Verkhovna Rada Vitali Klitschko, artist and Eurovision winner Ruslana, politician Arseniy Yatsenyuk, and several journalists (Horbyk 2019), all of whom made frequent speeches from the stage (see also Orlova 2016; Horbyk 2017, 23ff.; Voronova 2020).

This is followed by the fifth and last phase, in which the event fades and contemplation of and reflection on its implications take over. The fleeing of Yanukovych to Russia marked the total integration of the disruptive event into a transformative media event that could finally reach narrative closure with the signing of the EU association agreement on 27 June 2014. In the wake of this, however, another, more drawn-out story took over: the war that started with Russia's annexation of Crimea, the escalating armed conflict with Russia-backed separatists in the eastern parts of the country, the downing of Malaysian flight MH37 by a BUK surface-to-air missile, and Russia's full invasion of Ukraine in February 2022.

In some ways, the Euromaidan events followed the sequential structure, or narrative, proposed by media events theory, albeit with a disruption. This narrative does not have a single author but follows a pattern of narration that fits into Western narrative structures in a recognizable way, encoded (and decoded) within the cultural framework of storytelling into which we are socialized from an early age and that is an underlying matrix in our efforts to understand the world and shape it in an ordered, meaningful way. Although this narrative structure follows the general script laid out by media events theory, it also deviates in the details. The main deviance concerns the protagonists of the narrative, the key actors in the form of the ceremonial leaders who are executing the gestures and are the discursive drivers that structure the day-to-day microrituals during the third and fourth phases. In Dayan and Katz's examples, these leaders are mainly individuals—the pope visits Poland, Egyptian president Anwar Sadat visits Israel, and so forth. The Euromaidan Revolution, however, did not have one leader; rather, it was a collective action by the protesters.

A second deviation from the examples given in classic media events theory of "contests, conquests, and coronations" is the different media landscapes. To Dayan and Katz, media events are mainly a television genre. This is why they insist on the feature of preplanning outside of the media. However, they are not really consistent in their theorizing, and they actually touch briefly on phenomena that would not exist outside of television (or other media) at all. One of these is the Olympic Games, launched by Pierre de Coubertin in 1896 in their modern version and, from the beginning, an international competition wholly dependent on reporting by the press. Another example is the Eurovision Song Contest. We have argued elsewhere (Bolin 2010b) that this event is a good example of how media events can develop over time and fit into the world of the "media manifold," as Nick Couldry (2016) labels the contemporary world where media technologies are integrated into most, if not all, areas of social life. In this chapter we have largely followed Dayan and Katz's writings and pointed to the main functionality of these events as affirmative, offering societal integration—a "shared membership in a national or international community" (Dayan and Katz 1992, 197). But what is that community? In the next section we discuss the role of the Eurovision Song Contest in this wider narrative.

THE EUROVISION SONG CONTEST AS MEDIA EVENT
AND MEDIATIZED POLITICS

While Habermas focuses on the *intentionality* embedded in the act of communication and the intersubjective relations this act presupposes, Dayan and

Katz focus on the *functionality* of the narrated messages, the effects they might
have on societal integration and, indeed, their ability to instigate change. It is
hard to determine any commonly orchestrated intentions behind the narrated
events at Euromaidan, given the plurality of actors involved and the barely
controlled chaos in the midst of the revolution. In contrast, in the case of the
Eurovision Song Contest, the involved actors and their intentions are easier to
establish. First we provide some background on the contest, which might not
be familiar to non-European readers. We then discuss a few specific communication projects and their relation to the turbulent times from 2013 onward.

The Eurovision Song Contest is a Pan-European event where countries
compete to win the award for best song of the year. It has been organized
since 1956 by the European Broadcasting Union (EBU), the umbrella organization for Europe's public service broadcasters. The song contest attracts
huge audiences of several hundred million viewers in Europe and beyond,
including Australia, Israel, and Canada. Also at stake is that the winning
country gets to host the next year's final event. At least since 2002, the year
after Estonia won the contest (the first post-Soviet country to do so), the
ESC final had been used for branding purposes by the host country (see
Bolin 2002). However, it had not been as openly political as it was in 2017.

Ukraine has won the Eurovision Song Contest twice. Incidentally, these
two wins were close to two of its three revolutions, and both times Ukraine
took advantage of the event for purposes of public diplomacy and highly
politicized branding. In 2004, the same year as the Orange Revolution, artist
Ruslana won the ESC with her song "Wild Dances," and the following year
the competition was held in Kyiv. The new government was eager to make a
political statement about the break with the previous Russia-friendly regime
(Jordan 2015), and at the end of the contest, newly elected president Viktor Yuschenko presented the winner, Helena Paparizou from Greece, with
a special prize from the host country for "the song that unites the whole
Europe."[11] Yuschenko would have preferred to give a much longer speech,
but he was prevented from doing so by representatives of the EBU, which
wanted to keep politics out of the competition. Given the temptation to
reach hundreds of millions of European viewers in a live broadcast, the
EBU has not always been successful in this regard, and controversies over
song lyrics have been frequent. This occasion in 2005, however, was the
first time a head of state took advantage of the opportunity.

In 2016 Ukraine repeated its success with a highly politicized song. Representing Ukraine that year was singer Susana Jamaladyovna, whose stage

name is Jamala. Jamala, who is of Crimean Tatar descent, performed the song "1944," with lyrics about the deportation of hundreds of thousands of Tatars from Crimea to Siberia by the Soviet government under Joseph Stalin. The underlying message escaped few Europeans. The parallels to Russia's 2014 annexation of Crimea were obvious to all, including the European press, where it was widely discussed. Nobody was surprised when the Russian delegation protested and argued (unsuccessfully) that the song violated the EBU's nonpolitical policy.

The ambition to manage information in front of foreign audiences has not always been studied with a focus on cultural media events. Most often, research has focused on factual communications such as news and current affairs programs. However, it is also well established that the ESC, one of the world's largest "light" entertainment events, has political dimensions (Vuletic 2018), even if this usually takes the form of identity politics related to gender and sexuality.[12] But rarely has the contest's political nature been as obvious as when Ukraine hosted the event in Kyiv during the first two weeks of May 2017. This time, the ESC was being held in a European state at war.[13] Usually, the contest is an opportunity for all the participating countries to present attractive images of themselves to a mostly European audience. Host countries and cities, particularly those in the relatively new sovereign states in eastern Europe, often have high expectations, hoping that the attention will translate into more tourists and investors and perhaps an improved reputation as a "competent" European country. Thus, the ESC is more than just an entertaining television show; it is also an occasion for branding and exercising soft power (Raykoff and Tobin 2007). On this occasion, however, the host country had a problem: to attract audiences and tourists to Kyiv, the local organizers needed to convince visitors that it was safe.

In 2017 it was hardly obvious how the event could be utilized in the global market of attention (Davenport and Beck 2001). Was it an occasion for branding, or was it a platform to be used in the ongoing information war? Could it be both at the same time? Logically, the last option would be problematic. After all, branding a place is a matter of presenting an image that attracts foreign tourists or investors, which hardly seems likely if the country in question is involved in a violent conflict. Further, it was more than just a matter of choosing between two options—branding or propaganda—because the ESC is sponsored by the EBU, and host countries must conform to its regulations.

The dilemma facing the Ukrainian organizers was how to offer uncontroversial entertainment for an international audience (conforming to both

EBU regulations and Ukrainian branding intentions) while being involved in an ongoing conflict. The case of the ESC in Kyiv in 2017 reveals several contradictions between the apparently related concepts of soft power and propaganda (introduced and discussed in chapter 1).

MEGA EVENTS AND HABITATS OF MEANING

Planned mega events and festivals of various kinds—sports contests, cultural celebrations, business fairs, political rallies, popular music festivals—have become regular phenomena in contemporary societies across the globe (Delanty, Giorgi, and Sassatelli 2011; Roche 2002). These events attract attention not only in the locations where they are held but also, through mediation, on a much larger scale. In the contemporary world, these mega events are usually organized in cooperation with media outlets and produced primarily to be consumed by a media audience; thus they are often analyzed as media events (Dayan and Katz 1992; Couldry, Hepp, and Krotz 2010). Planned mega events may generate economic profit, create social cohesion, and be occasions where political messages are staged. Hence, a large festival or song contest is an attractive venue for a wide range of actors in corporate business (not only media businesses), state and city authorities, and political organizations and interest groups. And because these events are large and complex, many actors with highly diverse interests need to collaborate in the arrangement. No wonder these events are often prone to contradictions or disputes. In a sense, it is hardly surprising that we find a paradox in the Kyiv ESC.

Thus, people involved in the ESC do not always sing in the same key. In Kyiv, it was perfectly clear that various actors had divergent views of how and why the song contest was being held and, more fundamentally, what it was all about. As Erving Goffman famously said, related to his writing on frame analysis: "What is play for the golfer is work for the caddy" ([1974] 1986, 8). Likewise, for some people, the ESC is a project of European integration; for others, it is an occasion to promote a particular country or city. Some see it as an opportunity to enhance business or professional careers, while others see it as a key event within a specific fan culture (e.g., LGBTQ). Simultaneously, for most people, the ESC is probably just a matter of popular entertainment—which may be enjoyed, tolerated, or despised.

How do we make sense of these different views from actors participating in or consuming the same event? A rather obvious starting point is to recognize that people and organizations involved in a mega event are collaborating from positions that do not belong to the same "habitat of meaning," to use a concept suggested by Ulf Hannerz (2016, 135–160). Actors belonging to state authorities, the market, voluntary organizations, or some particular subculture in society do not always see things in the same light. Importantly, as emphasized by Hannerz, these habitats of meaning may or may not overlap partially or entirely. Thus, it seems perfectly reasonable for a Eurovision fan to be a patriot of a particular nation, sporting both an EU flag and a rainbow symbol on his jacket, while working with a commercial PR bureau on a subcontract for the city municipality—and in all capacities involved with the ESC. (This hypothetical person is not entirely invented.)

THE CONTEXT

In May 2016 Jamala took the stage at the Globe Arena in Stockholm as act number 21 in that year's ESC final. Dressed in a dark blue gown, she wore a haunted expression on her face as she started to sing: "When strangers are coming, they come to your house. They kill you all and say: We are not guilty, not guilty." Once the jury and the viewers had cast their votes, Jamala was declared the winner of the contest, much to the surprise of many ESC experts, who had predicted that Russian singer Sergei Lazarev would win. It was obvious to all who listened to the song and saw the performance that the lyrics referred to Russia's annexation of Crimea two years earlier. Russia, of course, alleged that the song violated the ESC policy that "No lyrics, speeches, gestures of a political or similar nature shall be permitted during the ESC."[14] The EBU, however, had reviewed the song beforehand and found that it did not break the rules.

Jamala's win meant that the following year's ESC would be held in Ukraine. Russian authorities and public commentators did not take this lightly. According to reports in the European mass media, Russian officials were irritated, dismissing the Ukrainian victory as unfair and illegitimate and contributing to a general demonization of Russia (*Telegraph* 2016). The state-controlled Russian TV channel RT ran a story titled "Eurovision Song Contest Funded by TV License Fee System that Criminalizes Poor People."[15]

For Ukraine, the importance of this victory extended far beyond the sphere of popular TV entertainment. When Jamala returned to Kyiv in triumph, she was welcomed by President Petro Poroshenko, who presented her with an Honored Artist of Ukraine award and assured her that her victory would contribute to the quick return of Crimea. "Virtually, the entire world has risen in support of Ukraine," said the president, according to news reports (Interfax Ukraine 2016). It was clear that the ESC, a light entertainment mega event, had become a factor in the management of information involving Russia and Ukraine. This role would continue throughout the year, leading up to the 2017 ESC final.

There were multiple actors involved in the drama that followed. The EBU and the national Ukrainian TV channel NTU (reorganized as a public broadcaster and renamed UA:PBU in 2017), were in charge of planning and organizing the event. Under their command were a number of subdepartments, working groups, subcontractors, and partners dealing with practical preparations and negotiations. Ukrainian government authorities affiliated with several ministries were influential in various stages of the process. So was the Kyiv municipality, which had a number of departments and contractors working on issues related to the event. Domestic and international media organizations were following the activities surrounding the planning of the next ESC. At the center of attention were reports of Russian actions and reactions at various points during the year. In addition, several voluntary organizations and political groups took part in shaping the upcoming event.

In addition to the above-mentioned actors were the event producers and technical staff—a mobile group of mostly non-Ukrainian individuals (a disproportionate number of them Swedish) and subcontractors, many of whom had been involved with the ESC in several cities over the years. Since the contest in Tallinn, Estonia, in 2002, the ESC had become an increasingly professionalized circus, with the same producers and technical staff touring Europe with their well-oiled machinery adept at organizing large-scale, live-broadcast media events (Bolin 2009, 2010b). The elements of the ESC that changed each year, besides the competing artists, were the national logotypes and slogans.

For the EBU and the professional producers and technicians, it was important that this year's ESC be business as usual, with as little interference as possible from the current political and military conflict. Actors on the Ukrainian state level may have been a bit ambivalent. On the one hand, a smoothly executed ESC final would be beneficial for Ukraine's image as an attractive and professional country. On the other hand, and mindful of President Poroshenko's reaction to Jamala's victory in Stockholm, it was tempting to see this as an opportunity to gain international support in a time of armed conflict.

Almost immediately after Jamala's return to Ukraine after her victory, rumors started to circulate in the international media. The first concerned the financial implications. Hosting the ESC involves substantial economic obligations from the national broadcasting company as well as from the state budget and the host city. Could Ukrainian authorities cover the costs when the country was engaged in a war and the domestic economy was in ruins? This was not an unreasonable question and one that had been posed to previous hosts from the former Soviet bloc, starting with Estonia in 2002 (Ericson 2002). The organizers in Ukraine promptly denied that there was any doubt about their ability to host the competition, just as the Estonian organizers had (Victoria Romanova, NTU deputy director general, interview, 21 October 2016). Still, rumors were circulating in the Russian and European media that the EBU was secretly planning for an alternative location and that Moscow was a possible substitute host city. This was also one of the first times Russia was accused of interfering in the arrangements by spreading "fake news."

StopFake reported numerous instances of the Russian media publishing stories that it regarded as false. StopFake director Yevhen Fedchenko claimed this was all part of a Russian strategy to discredit Ukraine: "We had, I would say, almost every week one fake piece of news on Eurovision" (interview, 11 May 2017). On its webpage, StopFake debunked claims that Ukrainian citizens would have to pay for Eurovision on their electric bills, that stray dogs were being killed on the streets of Kyiv, and that homeless people were being forced to move out of the city to clean it up before the event.

Although StopFake has close connections to government ministries (particularly the Ministry of Foreign Affairs), its debunking of news related to the ESC was apparently not coordinated with other Ukrainian actors. According to Fedchenko, they had pondered the possibility of sharing their view of Russian propaganda with visiting journalists at the press center of the Eurovision venue, but the local organizers (from the Ukrainian TV station) did not want to "politicize" the event more than necessary by inviting StopFake. "After all," Fedchenko said, "counterpropaganda can also be considered as propaganda" (interview, 11 May 2017).

The main Russian intervention in the upcoming event was not a fake story but something Ukrainian authorities interpreted as a deliberate provocation. Initially, Russia had threatened to boycott the contest due to the perceived politicization of the event by Ukraine. However, in March 2017 the Russian state-controlled Channel One announced the artist who would be representing the country in Kyiv: Yuliya Samoilova, a young female singer with a neuromuscular disorder that kept her confined to a wheelchair. Samoilova had been in the final of the Russian adaptation of *X Factor* in 2013 and had also performed at the opening of the 2014 Sochi Winter Paralympics. The problem was that Samoilova had also performed in Crimea in 2015, violating Ukrainian law by entering the occupied territory via Russia. She was therefore automatically banned from visiting Ukraine. Russian spokesperson Dmitry Peskov made assurances that Russia wanted "to avoid politicizing the Eurovision contest," as this "was absolutely unacceptable as far as the development of this international contest is concerned" (BBC News 2017). However, few believed that the Russians were unaware of the predicament caused by their choice of artist.

Ukrainian authorities were faced with a dilemma: either they could overlook Samoilova's crime and grant her special permission to participate in the contest, or they could uphold the ban and be seen as acting inhumanely toward a disabled girl. By selecting Samoilova for the Kyiv ESC, Russia communicated two contradictory messages simultaneously: Russia was no longer boycotting the song contest, which made the EBU happy, but it was deliberately causing trouble by selecting an artist Ukraine obviously could not accept. Furthermore, the context of the proposition made it impossible for Ukrainian authorities to avoid making a choice: they had to accept Samoilova or not. Ukraine was thus between a rock and a hard place: no matter how the country acted, there would be a downside.[16]

Ultimately, Ukraine refused Samoilova entrance to the country. The EBU tried, unsuccessfully, to convince Ukrainian authorities to let the Russian artist perform in Kyiv. Instead, Ukraine offered Russia the option of having Samoilova compete by video link from Moscow. Russia rejected that option and withdrew from the contest.

DESIGNING THE CONTEST

An important part of mega events is the choice of a theme and the creation of a design concept. The concept includes a slogan to express the theme and visual graphics to be used in all promotional materials. This became a critical phase in Ukraine. The national broadcaster had to come up with a concept that was acceptable to both the EBU and state and local authorities; it had to conceptualize something particularly Ukrainian and at the same time conform to ESC standards. Eventually, two PR and advertising companies took charge of this work (after a tender process). They initially suggested either "Celebrate Unity" or "Celebrate Harmony" as the slogan. People in the organization committee objected because, in the current situation, "unity" could be interpreted as a political comment on the Russian annexation of Crimea, and a country at war could hardly be described as a place of "harmony." After some pondering, "Celebrate Diversity" was chosen as the slogan, conforming to ESC values as well as Ukrainian branding intentions.

"Celebrate Diversity" obviously had a double meaning. First, it connoted sexual diversity, thus appealing to the large queer following and fan base the ESC has attained over the years. Second, it alluded to the motto of the European Union: "United in Diversity."[17] The EU motto "signifies how Europeans have come together, in the form of the EU, to work for peace and prosperity, while at the same time being enriched by the continent's many different cultures, traditions and languages."[18] Aligning with this motto can be seen as embracing the implied respect for the "relatively independent national identity and mutually exclusive political authority of each member state" in the EU (Fornäs 2012, 106) and as opposing the perceived pressure from Russia to conform to the hierarchical demands from the main player in the Eurasian Economic Community (which became the Eurasian Economic Union in May 2014). Building a closer alliance with the latter was seemingly President Yanukovych's intention when he abruptly refrained from signing the association agreement with the EU, triggering the protests that would eventually become the Revolution of Dignity.[19] However, the message implicit in the slogan "Celebrate Diversity" did not lead to any protests. Most likely, the stronger allusion to sexual diversity obscured the link to diversity within the European Union.

Four distinct ideas for graphic illustrations were presented to the organization committee, most of which were turned down. One was deemed too bright, too easygoing, and "too Brazilian" for Ukraine. Another, consisting of fireflies, was rejected for being too childish. Ultimately, the committee chose a concept inspired by a traditional Ukrainian necklace, consisting of a string of beads in different patterns. However, other actors were critical. Some pointed out that the patterns of some beads resembled the roof of an Orthodox church in Moscow and hence looked more Russian than Ukrainian. Another problem was the choice of magenta red and deep blue as the colors. Some critics thought yellow and blue (the colors of the Ukrainian flag) would be more appropriate. Others thought the blue was too dark and could be mistaken for black—black and red being the colors representing the Ukrainian Far Right (e.g., Pravyi Sektor). A third point of criticism was that the necklace was traditionally worn only by destitute people, signaling that Ukraine was a poor country. A group of prominent social activists even sent a letter to the EBU expressing these complaints and suggesting an alternative graphic concept—without success.

POLITICIZED EFFORTS

Some of the social activists participating in the protest over the design had been involved in Ukraine's nation branding efforts over the last fifteen years (see Bolin and Ståhlberg 2015; Ståhlberg and Bolin 2016). Among them was the managing director of CFC Consulting—also the initiator of the Ukraine Crisis Media Center. CFC had offered its services to the ESC organizers but secured only a minor contract with the national television company and the Kyiv municipality. However, CFC's work also included some of the more politicized efforts, which were highly visible in the city during the ESC week.

One of CFC's creations was an enormous poster covering the façade of the huge trade union building on Maidan—a building completely burned out during the turbulent days of 2013–2014. The poster read "Freedom is our religion," above an image of a breaking steel chain and a blue sky (figure 4.2). It made no reference to the ESC, but it was clearly a deliberate effort to remind visitors to Kyiv and to the famous square what was really going on—that is, there was more at stake than a song contest (Goffman [(1974) 1986] uses the term "keying" for the practice of directing interpretation toward a particular frame of understanding).

Another installation, even more photographed and debated than the poster, could be seen just a few hundred meters from the square (figure 4.3). On a hill above the Dnieper River stands an arch erected in 1982, during Soviet times, to commemorate the sixtieth anniversary of the USSR. It is called the People's Friendship Arch, a typical Soviet monument representing the brotherhood of the Russian and Ukrainian peoples. But during the ESC, it was renamed the Arch of Diversity and painted to resemble a rainbow (see Gerdes 2017). It was, of course, an obvious but humorous provocation directed toward Russia—a country that had enacted "anti-homo

Figure 4.2
Poster covering the façade of the trade union building on Maidan Nezalezhnosti.
Photo by authors, May 2017

propaganda" laws beginning in 2006 (Wilkinson 2014). However, it was not appreciated by all Ukrainians: right-wing members of parliament from the Svoboda Party protested this celebration of queerness, and the painting of the rainbow was halted before completion (Ukraine Crisis Media Center 2017). However, claimed one of the creators, "the job was already done." The effort was a success, as images of the rainbow arch had nearly gone viral on the internet.

The rainbow colors were removed after the ESC festival ended in May. The Friendship Arch, however, has continued to be the focus of semiotic commentary about cracks in the friendship between the Russian and Ukrainian peoples. A couple of years later, someone painted a small crack on top of the arch, subtly indicating the ongoing tensions between the two nations (figure 4.4).

The last example of the politicized initiatives by this group of activists was seen only on the internet. CFC Consulting hastily produced the official promotional video for ESC 2017. It shows a small girl—Anastasiya Baginska,

Figure 4.3
The Arch of Diversity: People's Friendship Arch in Cross Park, Kyiv, during
Eurovision Song Contest week, May 2017.
Photo by authors

who represented Ukraine in the Junior ESC in November 2017—singing a
catchy song titled "We Won't Give Up" and dancing through picturesque
Ukrainian landscapes and the streets of Kyiv while large, patterned beads
(from the logo) are rolled or carried around.[20] There is nothing remarkable
about this video, except for the last scene: The girl is pictured on a sailing boat
on the wide open sea against a bright blue sky. She looks up, the wind in
her hair, and waves her hand toward an impressive castle built on a high cliff
overlooking the sea. To most viewers of the video, this is simply a spectacular
castle in a beautiful and dramatic landscape. However, to many Ukrainians
and Russians, it is recognizable as the Swallow's Nest, a famous tourist attraction on Crimea. Russia had occupied the peninsula since 2014, as noted by a
few commentators on YouTube.[21] An audience with that knowledge could
easily understand the provocation in the song title: "We Won't Give Up."

A core issue related to using the ESC as a platform for managing information and playing with signifiers is that it was unclear to what extent these

Figure 4.4
Cracks in the friendship: People's Friendship Arch in Cross Park, Kyiv, 1 October 2019.
Photo by authors

efforts were linked to the intentions and strategies of either Ukrainian ESC organizers or government authorities. In other contexts, the national TV broadcaster avoided politicizing the event. The Kyiv municipality sponsored various other activities and PR initiatives around the city, but all of them were very touristy and lacked a politically offensive tone. CFC displayed initiative and creativity, but it was unclear who commissioned the freedom poster, the rainbow arch, and the promotional video.

The same question surrounds the decision to have the electro-folk band Onuka perform as an interval act in the final. Onuka mixes traditional Ukrainian instruments such as the sopilka, bandura, and buhay with high-tech electronic instruments to form a kind of avant-garde pop music.[22] This might not be controversial in itself: all countries that host the ESC display a certain amount of folklore and nationalist symbols in their interval acts. However, Onuka explicitly forefronts its traditional Ukrainian musical roots and the revival of musical traditions suppressed during Soviet times. It is hard to tell whether Onuka's performance should be seen as a political statement, but as an element in the wider discourse on the tensions between Ukraine and Russia, it becomes one piece in the mosaic constructed around the ESC.

This lack of clarity about the coordination of the various efforts to manage communication also raises the question of what kind of meaning management this really was. None of the CFC's projects during the ESC could be understood as the simple transmission of clear-cut messages. For most people attending the song contest in Kyiv, it would be hard to understand how these efforts related to the Ukraine-Russia war. The "Freedom is our religion" poster may have been a reminder of the recent upheaval on the square, but it was expressed in a very general way and with a rather uncontroversial formulation, resembling the usual nonpolitical slogans from the EBU. Probably only people who were already aware of the situation caught the provocative nature of the message—that the Euromaidan Revolution had liberated Ukraine from its chains to Russia. The meaning behind the Arch of Diversity was even more obscure to anyone who understood it mainly as a tribute to the ESC and its large gay audience and was unaware of the original message of friendship between the Russian and Ukrainian peoples. Likewise, the promotional video required local knowledge of geography to be understood as politically controversial. And judging from the comments on YouTube, this message escaped nearly everyone.

These three efforts seemingly had political intentions and could be seen as an orchestrated form of strategic narrative. They were also ambiguous, playful, humorous, and witty, despite the fact that their messages were hard to interpret for all but a small group of cognoscenti. There was clearly an element of mischievousness in this form of meaning management. These communications carried a double meaning and could be understood as both banal and serious—or soft and toxic—depending on who was listening (see chapter 1) and from what particular habitat of meaning. In a sense, these efforts to take advantage of the ESC as an opportunity for political communication reflected how Russian authorities sought to manage meaning ambiguously when choosing Samoilova to compete in the song contest.

CONCLUSION: TROLLING OUTSIDE THE INTERNET

In June 2021 we were again reminded of the crafty forms of meaning management related to the Ukraine-Russia situation. Like the Eurovision Song Contest, the context was one not usually regarded as political: a large sports event. The European soccer championship, organized by the Union of European Football Associations (UEFA), should have taken place in 2020, but because of the COVID-19 pandemic, it had been rescheduled. Ukraine's national team had qualified to compete, and so had Russia's. On 6 June, just a few days before the championship was about to start, the president of the Ukrainian football association, Andrij Pavelko, presented a new design for the team's shirts.[23] The shirts were the usual blue and yellow of the Ukrainian flag, but a few design details had been added. On the front was a map of Ukraine that included the Russian-occupied Crimean Peninsula and the war zones of the Donbas region. In addition, two slogans were printed on the shirt: *Slava Ukraini!* (Glory to Ukraine) and *Heroyam slava!* (Glory to the heroes). Both slogans had been used by protesters during the Euromaidan Revolution.

A picture of the new team shirt was posted on the Facebook page of the Ukrainian Football Association and reported by the Ukrainian media. This immediately aroused reactions from Russian politicians, who saw the shirt as a political provocation. The *Guardian* quoted a Russian parliamentarian who claimed that showing a map of Ukraine "which includes a Russian territory is illegal," and a spokesperson for the Russian Foreign Ministry was quoted as saying that the two slogans echoed a Nazi rallying cry. Support came, however, from the US embassy in Ukraine, which stated on Twitter: "Love the new look! Glory to Ukraine!" (Roth 2021).

The UEFA approved the shirt design, with one exception: the slogan "Glory to the heroes" had to be removed. Neither the map of Ukraine nor the second slogan caused any objections. After all, the annexation of Crimea has not been acknowledged internationally, and the United Nations still considers it Ukrainian territory. The expression *Slava Ukraini!* predates the Euromaidan Revolution, as does *Heroyam slava!* (Chraibi 2016). The outcome of the protest was entirely predictable. However, the incident was similar to the Russians' attempt to launch Yuliya Samoilova as their ESC contestant—a strategic communication act that forced Ukraine to respond in an unfavorable way. Similarly, producing a map of Ukraine including Crimea—a statement that violated Russian law—forced Russia's official representatives to respond with a protest. Everyone, including the Russians, knew the protest would be rejected, but for the Russian delegation, not protesting was not a realistic option. Like Ukraine's rejection of Samoilova, this time Russia was forced to take an unpopular position. In the contemporary lingo of the online world, both these acts are examples of internet "trolling," as is the painting of the Friendship Arch in rainbow colors and the depiction of Swallow's Nest in the promotional video.

The degrees of strategic intentionality behind these moves, based on the material at our disposal, cannot be determined. Such a determination would be required to establish this type of communication as strategic, deceptive, or manipulative. Although an analysis in line with Habermas's ([1981] 1992) theory of communicative action is beyond the scope of this chapter, we can convincingly point to the functionality of information management, in line with media events theory discussed earlier. In the final chapter, we discuss the complexities of informational and meaning management at greater length.

THE INFORMATIONAL STATE IN TURBULENT TIMES

In an increasingly globalized and mediatized world, information management and policy take new forms, involve new agents, and are managed on new communication platforms. This means that the power and control of information are becoming more diffused. The rise of large-scale transnational media companies undermines nation-states' previous monopolies on the control of information. Access to media production technologies by nongovernmental actors such as corporations, civil society organizations, and individual citizens makes it easier to bypass traditional gatekeepers such as news media outlets. Furthermore, the flow of people between corporations and governmental departments introduces new practices and communication strategies.

We set out to analyze and discuss the management of information and meaning in turbulent times. For the nation-state of Ukraine, times have indeed been turbulent since the collapse of the Soviet Union. The nature and character of these turbulent times are described differently, however, depending on who the storyteller is. One major account holds that the country has experienced three revolutions in as many decades. Another position is that Ukraine has been hijacked by western European forces, even fascists, to split the Eurasian power bloc.[1] These positions all build on various ways of narrating events. All acts of communication do not, however, form narratives—especially if one insists, as we do, that the concept of narrative is reserved for "temporally ordered stories" with causal relations between events, agents, and contexts (Fornäs 2017, 13). Social reality is seldom ordered in the same clear and logical way as mediated narratives are. The narrative is, in fact, the means by which we, as social subjects, make sense of the surrounding and increasingly complex, ambivalent, and sometimes contradictory character of social reality in the twenty-first century.

In this chapter we summarize our empirical analysis of the agents, media forms, and events examined in the previous chapters, and we discuss the wider theoretical implications this provokes. Although we focus on Ukraine, we also argue that some of the theoretical implications of the events there resonate with other contexts and have wider significance for our understanding of developments elsewhere. We start by recapping our main empirical findings, which leads to a discussion of the implications for traditional media theory. We argue in favor of holistic perspectives on how different media forms and technologies interact with one another and help circulate images, text snippets, and even full narratives. We are not the first to do this; there are plenty of earlier examples, including some of our own writings. However, we believe this is an important point to reiterate, since it is easy to call for researchers to be more holistic in their understanding of contemporary media landscapes but much more difficult to suggest *how* to do so. Next, we critically examine the usefulness of the concept of narrative and, with the help of our empirical material and our findings from Ukraine, explain why it is important with respect to a distinct conceptualization of narrative and in relation to *other* concepts that struggle to describe the contemporary communicative universe. We also argue for the importance of learning across subdisciplines. Just as we have learned tremendously from stepping out of our comfort zone and entering uncharted territory, we welcome more cross-disciplinary encounters. Modern science tends to be specialized, and a disadvantage of this trend is that sometimes things develop in discursive ponds, where they would benefit from swimming in the same pool. We end the book with some reflections about how the Ukraine story has been narrated and how this narration resonates with older forms of constructing revolutionary events.

AGENTS, MEDIA TECHNOLOGIES, AND COMMUNICATION GENRES

In previous chapters we accounted for the "barely controlled chaos" in the Ukrainian media landscape (Gupta 2012, 14). We showed how the plurality of individual and organizational agents within journalism, public relations, corporations, governments, and civil society, with different but connected backgrounds, contribute to the largely disorganized yet surprisingly unified information activities in support of Ukraine. It can be argued that, taken together, these activities make up a somewhat coherent policy regarding how the country should be communicated. One might have imagined that the Ministry of Information Policy served as a hub around which all these activities were coordinated, given that organized networks need some form of centralized or hierarchical organization (see Rossiter 2006). Yet this was hardly the case. Instead, the MIP was one of many agents participating in the endeavor to manage information and meaning. The connections between the various organizational agents were largely personal ones— kind of like social bonds on the individual level, or what Pierre Bourdieu ([1983] 1986) would have called "social capital." As Bourdieu (1996) points out, social capital is often acquired through connections and friendships developed in educational environments, and many of our informants have educational institutions in common. For example, the National University of Kyiv-Mohyla Academy—one of the smaller universities in Kyiv (and in Ukraine)—has played a prominent role in the various turbulent events since the collapse of the Soviet Union. In particular, the Business Administration and Journalism Departments are two central hubs from which several of our informants graduated and where some are also lecturing.

All these connections and social bonds produce a kind of *multiplication of the state*, where information policy is distributed over multiple agents in a very loosely coordinated way. This multiplication takes the form of the distribution of state functions, which appear to be delegated to civil society and corporate agents alike, with the state taking minimal organizational responsibility. A delegation always involves two parties: one who delegates and one who receives the power to act on behalf of those who delegate. Like Bourdieu, we could ask on whose mandate all these agents are speaking and acting discursively "in the name of the social whole" (Bourdieu [2012] 2020, 45). Bourdieu presumes that the agents acting in the name of the state have been given a mandate, but in the Ukrainian case, it is unclear who is authorizing strategic action, since the Ukrainian state is both weak and distrusted by other agents with "communication power" (Castells 2009).

Who authorizes agents to speak in the name of the nation-state is far from obvious in Ukraine, but perhaps this informality is functional and is a model through which the neoliberal state works in the present informational society. Post-Soviet countries with short histories of independence have had to rebuild their state functions from scratch; they wanted to rid themselves of the burdensome past and thus looked for organizational models of the most advanced and modern kind. Thus, Estonia "leapfrogged" its communication system, undertaking a rapid expansion of the digital and largely mobile infrastructure to become a front-runner in digital society (see Braman 2006, 37). This was also the case with regard to the digitalization of the economy and electronic financial transactions. Perhaps what we are seeing in Ukraine is the rise of a new type of informational state in which the organization of information policy is decentered along network principles, where many nodes are connected but there is no hierarchy. Our material does not permit us to draw accurate conclusions, but the question is well worth following up with future research about the organizational forms of information, meaning, and policy management in the informational state.

The various agents involved in information and meaning management are operating on different technological platforms, so one can also speak about a *multiplication of media technologies* when telling the Ukrainian story. Large national and international mass media organizations are increasingly dependent on niche media such as streamed audiovisual services, online social media, and presentational digital media such as PowerPoint and Prezi. However, even less obvious media and presentational forms, such as museum exhibitions, restaurant interior designs, and monuments, are taken advantage of for commentary in public spaces and contribute "affective images" (Eder 2017). Even the design of football teams' uniforms can, under specific circumstances, work as affective media, contribute to the discursive framing of events, and provoke debate, arouse feelings, and stir up emotions.

However, we can also observe a *multiplication of communication genres* ranging from journalism and news (StopFake, Euromaidan Press) to PR and branding (CFC, Banda, Republique) to information and official statements and communiqués (MIP, UCMC). All these are relatively traditional genres, and within them several narratives have been constructed around Ukraine—of revolution and resistance, but also of corruption and conflict. Communicative efforts can take less conventional forms, such as graffiti and decorations of monuments and buildings in public spaces. These are less structured and do not really form coherent narratives; rather, they are bundles of signs that form assemblages of meaning, but not necessarily in narrative form because they lack the quality of temporal order. It is important to distinguish between narratives and other forms of semiotic or discursive expression, and as we have repeatedly pointed out, we wish to reserve the conceptual toolbox of narrative analysis for those temporally structured fictional or documentary texts that tell about social and media events.

The multiplication of agents, technologies, and genres involved in the management of information and meaning since Ukraine's independence in 1991 provokes a number of questions related to media theory and narratology and, ultimately, about statehood, the informational state, and information policy. In the following sections we deal with each of these issues as they are affected by our empirical observations.

MEDIA TECHNOLOGIES AND INTERCONNECTED, DYNAMIC MEDIA LANDSCAPES

Media and communication research has always privileged certain media technologies over others, and the conceptual understanding of various forms of communication has therefore neglected certain media. Take, for example, a classic definition of mass communication such as the one proposed by Charles Wright in his short book *Mass Communication* (1959, 13ff.). To Wright, mass communication is characterized by the "nature of the audience" (large, heterogeneous, and anonymous), the "nature of the communication experience" (public, rapid, and transient), and the "nature of the communicator" (organized). Based on this definition, it is obvious that Wright prioritized the press, radio, and television, rather than other media at the time. Cinema and recorded music were, for example, communicated to anonymous mass audiences; they were also transient and produced by industrialized cultural producers. But this was seemingly irrelevant to Wright. This bias has continued in the study of mass communication, and it is our argument that the multiplication of communication technologies in the media landscape, in addition to the multiple agents that can produce text, sound, and images, means that communication processes must be studied as more complex endeavors. Messages, images, and narratives are constructed synchronously *across* different media as multiplatform texts—for example, in storytelling, where the narrative parts may be spread out over television, online games, websites, and mobile applications, and where the combination of narrative units contributes to the whole. However, messages are also formed diachronically through the successive circulation *between* platforms, where narratives or parts of narratives are molded while traveling between different media technologies.

Meaningful messages thus travel between niche and mass media and vice versa. During this circulation, messages transform, take on new meanings, and are stripped of previous meanings when recontextualized. Circulation always includes all the various moments of the communication process, where meaningful messages are constantly constructed, reconstructed, recontextualized, and interpreted as meaningful during the encoding and decoding process. This is perhaps most obvious in relation to the various branding efforts in Ukraine, where an analysis of the presentational media such as PowerPoint and Prezi in which messages are initially formed has illustrated how images and text snippets circulate between public and semipublic spheres of communication. However, it is equally important to examine how narratives were constructed around the Euromaidan events in the flow back and forth between social media, niche media, and mass media from late November 2013 to February 2014.

The fact is that media users are surrounded by more and more media technologies and means of communication, and arguing that media research should develop more holistic understandings of the media landscape is not novel. As early as the 1940s, Harold Lasswell (1948) argued the same point about doing holistic analysis, but he also acknowledged the burden this would put on researchers (and research funding). However, these arguments have been revived in the digital world of interconnected media, and in this context we are thinking about researchers such as Nick Couldry (2016), using the concept of "media manifold"; Mirca Madianou and Daniel Miller (2011), who work with the concept of "polymedia"; and José van Dijck, Thomas Poell, and Martijn de Waal (2018), who prefer the concept of "media ecology." In our own writings we have cited the benefits of the concept of "media landscape" because it indicates a structure produced through human agency, rather than an organically grown ecology (Bolin 2003, 2006a, 2017). What we could add to this discussion is perhaps a deeper understanding of the interrelations among media technologies and how images, texts, and fragments circulate between them. This should lead to the study of not only how media technologies are interconnected but also *what types of content* are interconnected and circulated through them and how that interconnectedness affects the narratives and images that are ultimately widely circulated among media audiences and users.

MANAGEMENT OF INFORMATION, MEANING, AND NARRATION

Our point of departure was grounded in a theoretical distinction between the management of information and the management of meaning. In chapter 2 we posited that to manage meaning one must have some idea of how meaning is produced in the receiving part of the communication chain. This could very well be related to the concept of soft power, which builds on the idea of having people align with a particular ideological conception of the world. Management of meaning can be achieved only if the communication effort has a deliberate intention. Management of information is a more descriptive concept. Agents manage information without intentionality in many situations. In today's society, data are the main drivers of the world economy and the main business model of large platform companies such as Facebook, Google, and Amazon. Every day agents amass and process data without thinking about how these data will be used or for what reason. But they nonetheless manage information—compile it, refine it, store it, archive it, and so on. Information management, then, does not necessarily involve intentionality on the part of the information manager. To manage meaning is something else. It includes thinking about expected outcomes, results, and success (for one's own cause) or failure (for the counterpart, if the situation is constructed as antagonistic). In theories of international relations, many situations involving strategic communication are indeed constructed as antagonistic. For example, the basic idea behind soft power as a practice is ontologically antagonistic: someone has to be convinced, and the task of soft power, public diplomacy, and strategic narratives is to produce the type of consent needed. In that sense, these practices differ very little, if at all, from the manufacturing of consent and the propaganda model theorized by Edward Herman and Noam Chomsky (1988). Soft power and strategic narratives are thus approaches that presuppose a polarized world of conflicting interests where consensus can be achieved only through the strategic action of manipulation and discursive deception (see Habermas [1976] 1979), and foreign policy success depends on "whose story wins," as Joseph Nye (2010) defines the aim of soft power (quoted in Szostek 2018, 72). But if the ultimate goal of storytelling is to win, it is hard not to see that activity in terms of ideological work and the production of submission through persuasion.

This is where we can contribute to the literature of strategic narratives. Strategic narratives are defined by their main proponents as "a means for political actors to construct a shared meaning of the past, present, and future of international politics to shape the behaviour of domestic and international actors" (Miskimmon, O'Loughlin, and Roselle 2013, 2).[2] To us, a view of narrative as part of an antagonistic discursive struggle seems too instrumental, since it perceives communication as a means by which other than simple communicative aims are strived for. For communications practitioners, this is, of course, their business, whether they are working in the field of commercial branding or nation branding and whether they want to form public opinion, instigate hatred and confusion, or mobilize loyalty. Our approach is analytically broader, and we have sought to understand how communication works, how it is organized, and what the implications are for communication in turbulent times such as those in Ukraine. Accordingly, some features of the strategic communication approach fit less well with our observations.

A focus on the strategic dimension of narrative must, by necessity, build on the intentionality of the sender, the individual who constructs the message and directs it to a target audience with a specific aim in mind. Our previous experience, as well as our research for this specific project, reveals that communication does not work in such a straightforward way. First, the encoding moment is much messier, more complex, and disorganized, and it involves agents whose aims are not always compatible. At best, they are similar, and the "text as meaningful discourse" is coherent enough to privilege a certain kind of meaning over others (Hall 1973). At worst, the polysemic nature of affective images makes them so open to interpretation that the strategy behind their production can hardly be established in any meaningful way. Strategic communication presupposes a unified agent at the encoding moment, and as we have shown, this is seldom the case. In times of open war, communication efforts may be more tightly integrated, but even on those occasions it is difficult to orchestrate all communication to speak in one voice. We believe this has been the case since the full-scale Russian invasion of Ukraine in February 2022.

Second, decades of audience research have persistently pointed out the spectrum of interpretations among those who make meaning out of narratives at the moment of decoding.[3] This is especially important to keep in mind when analyzing images and narratives that are disseminated internationally or interpreted by international audiences. Take the painted rainbow in Cross Park in Kyiv during the Eurovision Song Contest. It was seen by thousands of international visitors to the city and by many more people through mass and social media. To most of them, the rainbow message of gender and sexual diversity was the main takeaway. But to observers familiar with the origin of the People's Friendship Arch—a Soviet monument celebrating the friendship between the peoples of Russia and Ukraine—other layers of meaning were activated, including political meanings beyond the identity politics of gender and queerness. Even more subtle was the reference to the Swallow's Nest in the promotional video for the ESC. A quick look at the comments about the

YouTube clip reveals that many more viewers recognized the name of the young girl in the video than could identify the castle and its location on the shores of the Black Sea in the Russian-occupied Crimean Peninsula.

Third, we think a more fine-tuned distinction is needed between narratives—as texts organized into sequences that have internal causal interrelations in which actors, contexts, and events are ordered in a meaningful way—and textual fragments that might point to the narrative but are not part of it. With Gerard Genette (1997), we think of these fragments as *paratexts*, which sometimes enrich the narrative by contributing layers of meaning. Such "thresholds of interpretation" often work to close down the interpretation spectrum and provide *anchorage* for the text by adding meaningful signs and thus make them less polysemic. Paratexts can sometimes have narrative form, such as movie trailers or reviews. Many of them, however, are much less complex and do not contain a narrative structure, such as posters, ads, toys, stickers, and other promotional materials (see Gray 2010). The defining feature of paratexts is that they are not part *of* the narrative but point *to* it. In that sense, they also define the limits of the narrative—just as thresholds mark the boundary between one room and another.

It is thus worth reflecting on the many presentational forms that do not lean on narrative structure. Advertising, for example, works with other kinds of presentational forms to arouse desire among consumers. The combination of signs in branding and advertising is supposed to work with associative signs that point in various directions and connote distinct values, lifestyles, or identities. These are not necessarily presented as causal relationships between events, agents, or contexts, but they work through connotations relying on metaphor, metonym, synecdoche, and other types of textual features in the work of signifying practice (see, e.g., Goldman 1992).

A major difference between narrative and associative signs of communication is that narratives reduce the range of interpretations, whereas associative images and textual fragments are notoriously polysemic and carry several layers of meaning. Associative signs may point toward a particular narrative and sometimes make it richer, but they are also important sources of interpretation in their own right. Images, like words, can be sweet and evoke positive feelings, sentiments, and loyalties among their interpreters. Conversely, toxic images instigate disgust, anger, and hatred and fuel antipathy toward something or someone. Both kinds of affective images can be used for strategic communication purposes and in rhetorical communication.

As Jens Eder claims, "countless images . . . are being effective by being affective" (2016, 63). Moreover, strategic communicators may use images that are doubly coded; for instance, the same sign can be interpreted as either sweet or toxic, depending on the audience or on the competence of the observer. By sheer ambiguity, affective images may provoke confusion and instigate contagion in a social field (Gibbs 2008; Kølvraa 2015). The very point of affective images, one could claim, is that they do not offer a narrative. More often, affective communication destabilizes a political discourse.

Narratives have a temporal structure and, most often, a narrative closure, where the story is resolved and the *fabula*—the full story as a logical sequence of events—is completed. Some narratives, however, are open-ended, and certain presentational genres such as horror movies and pornography often rely on open endings (to permit the possibility of a sequel, should the narrative be a box-office hit). A recurring problem in the literature of strategic narratives is that sequences of events in the social world become conflated with the representations of these events in a sequential order to make up a fabula. For example, take Laura Roselle, Alister Miskimmon, and Ben O'Loughlin's (2014) example of the Cold War as a strategic narrative. The Cold War was an epoch during which the world's international power relations were centered on the opposition between the United States and the Soviet Union (and their respective allies). The Cold War can, of course, be narrativized and made into a novel or a feature film—the most iconic example, perhaps, being John Le Carré's (1963) *The Spy Who Came in from the Cold*. However, the novel and film are fictional representations of the Cold War, not the actual state of international relations that played out between the end of World War II and the fall of the Berlin Wall. Likewise, the sequence of events occurring around the Maidan in Kyiv in the winter of 2013–2014 was not a narrative; it *became* so by being understood as the last of three consecutive revolutions.

The reason Daniel Dayan and Elihu Katz's (1992) media events theory fits so well as narrative analysis is that the events they study are modeled on a narrative structure. Although the events are orchestrated outside of the media—albeit with the media already in mind at the point of planning—they follow a narrative segmentation from the start. The outcome of the Olympic Games is known beforehand: the dates are set and everybody knows that the games will end with someone, or some country, winning. Each country thus fulfills a function in the narrative, as Vladimir Propp theorizes. The fabula will be completed, although the dramatis personae are exchangeable, and each action is defined by its part in the narrative progression (Propp [1928] 1968, 19ff.). In these instances, social reality is not narrativized in representation; rather, social reality is structured along narrative conventions from the beginning. This works for preplanned events such as the Olympic Games, the Eurovision Song Contest, and state visits—all of which are scripted events. But it works less well for the Cold War.

From a more scientific-philosophical point of view, there is something interesting about the phenomenon of scientific terminology traveling between paradigms. The conceptual toolbox of narrative analysis was developed for analytical purposes and grew out of a specific ontological and epistemological understanding of what a text is and what it does. The wider context is structuralist (or poststructuralist) (see Barthes [1966] 1977). When that terminology is incorporated into praxis-oriented fields, such as international relations, the change in ontological presuppositions does something to the theory. Narrative analysis, as it was formulated by Propp ([1928] 1968) and in relation to popular fictional texts by Umberto Eco (1981) and Janice Radway ([1984] 1991), built on the idea of the "death of the author" and the "birth of the reader," as this break with intentionality was famously introduced by Roland Barthes ([1968] 1977). Questions of intentionality and effects were explicitly excluded from that epistemological framework, and the main point of narrative analysis was to study the relation between texts and readers. These readers could be implied, as in reader-response theory (e.g., Iser 1974), or they could be social subjects, as in media reception research (e.g., Hall 1973; Schrøder 2000) and media ethnography (e.g., Drotner 1994). Either way, the relation between the text and the interpreting subject is the focus of interest, and the author is at best a contextual factor. As the theory of strategic narratives aims to understand "an actor's strategic aims" (Miskimmon, O'Loughlin, and Roselle 2013, 8), this means that narrative analysis shifts the focus from readers to authors. This difference is significant for understanding *where* along the communication chain meaning is produced and whether meaning can be successfully programmed into a text to produce a unified response.

The theory of strategic narratives can be said to comprise two parts: one that is rhetorically slanted and focuses on intentionality, persuasive power, and goal fulfillment (effects), and another that seeks to understand how narratives are scripting behavior. The first part of this theory seems redundant to us, as if traditional strategic communication were dressed in a new evening gown. However, our mission is not to evaluate intentions among the sender but to ponder the consequences of textual forms and expressions, so we have not elaborated on this theory. And although we have plenty of empirical data from interviews with media producers and branding agents, this material does not allow a systematic analysis of intentions either.

The second part of the theory that seeks to understand how narratives are scripting behavior seems more interesting to us, as it deals with the power of representation over social orientation and social behavior. If we think of communication as texts, images, and narratives circulating among media platforms, it is clear that those engaged in the encoding of texts as meaningful discourse are also readers. Just as anyone who takes a picture from the internet, processes it in an editing program, and adds text to produce a meme is a "media produser" (Bruns 2006), professional producers of media texts pick and choose among the enormous archive available online. The principles of production are the same, although the resources and the distribution potentials might vary enormously.

Another interesting theoretical feature to ponder is the use of industry jargon incorporated as analytical concepts. This is the case with *nation branding*, which, as we have argued, is not an analytical concept but a stake in the discursive games among stakeholders. Nation branding is a practice, and at best, the concept works descriptively for certain types of activities in which PR and marketing professionals engage. If one wants to understand theoretically what type of communication the practice of nation branding employs, it is much better to use other toolboxes; for example, Jürgen Habermas's ([1981] 1991) theory of strategic communication provides better explanatory power. Contrary to communicative action, which aims at mutual understanding and consensus, strategic communication is a type of social action that is goal oriented, striving for success. It can be openly strategic or, as is most often the case, concealed, masking its aims and goals. Furthermore, this concealment can be unconscious, such as when agents relay information they believe is factually correct but is not (perhaps planted by someone intending to take advantage of "useful idiots"). But strategic communication can also be consciously deceptive, deliberately manipulating its audience.

Habermas's theory of strategic and communicative action builds on the speech act theory of John Austin ([1955] 1975) and John Searle (1969) and is modeled on face-to-face speech. One of the criticisms of Habermas is that he models his universal theory of communication on speech rather than on mediated communication (e.g., Alexander 1991). There is some truth to this criticism, and Habermas's theory does not fit all communicative situations that use media technologies. However, the most problematic part of his theory concerns the communicative action element, which supposedly has communicative understanding as its overarching purpose. His distinctions between different types of strategic action have garnered less criticism, and for the analysis of commercial branding and advertising, Habermas provides a valuable general model of explanation. However, because his focus is on the interrelation between communicating subjects, it needs to be expanded.

Pierre Bourdieu (1991), in *Language and Symbolic Power*, also bases his argument on speech act theory, but he insists that one must consider the institution that frames communication and gives the speaker the authority to communicate. Habermas is helpful for distinguishing acts of communication from one another in a fine-grained way, but for an analysis of communication executed on behalf of the state and that has received or appropriated the authority to speak as a representative of state institutions, it is especially important to have the institutional frameworks in mind. Despite their over-arching ontological differences—emphasizing consensus (Habermas) or domination and reproduction of power relations (Bourdieu)—the two can be combined, especially when it comes to strategic communication, information policy, and communication within the frameworks of the informational state, to which we turn next.

THE MEDIATED CENTER OF THE INFORMATIONAL STATE

The multiplicity of agents involved in Ukrainian information and meaning management begs the question: how can we think of Ukraine as an informational state? An informational state is one constituted by its mutually dependent networked and interdependent agents both public and private, all of which require "the global information infrastructure for information creation, processing, flows, and use" (Braman 2006, 36). But let us first ponder a more fundamental question: what is it that characterizes a state? Bourdieu, in his lectures on the state, refers to British sociologists Philip Corrigan and

Derek Sayer (1985), who point out that "states state"; they make "statements" and lay down "statutes" (quoted in Bourdieu [2012] 2020, 11). Relatedly, and around the same time, US legal scholar Laurence Tribe (1985) was discussing "the constitutive dimension of constitutional decisions: the fact that constitutional choices affect, and hence require consideration of, the way in which a polity wishes to constitute itself." We believe that the ways Ukraine is represented in the communicative acts described in preceding chapters are constitutive for the formation of the informational state of Ukraine, and we posit that we are seeing the Ukrainian informational state in its *becoming* in the present. In the next few paragraphs we unpack this proposition.

Bourdieu proposes that the "agents who have made the state, and have made themselves into state agents by making the state, have had to make the state in order to make themselves into the holders of power" (Bourdieu [2012] 2020, 38). This implies that state power is the result of struggles during which some agents appropriate positions as state agents—that is, those who represent the state and speak in its name. If this is true for contemporary Ukraine, the result would be a very distributed state in terms of information agency, considering the many individuals and organizations involved. The question of who has given all these agents a mandate to speak in the name of the nation is also unclear. One way to see it is that a mandate is not given but taken or appropriated. The "barely controlled chaos" (Gupta 2012) between late November 2013 and late February 2014 opened up a space for various agents to act, using the affordances of various media and communication technologies to constitute the conditions under which state formation can be built. Chaos is a state in which irrationality seems to reign (see Braman, 2021), but chaos and turbulence also present opportunities for the reconstitution of things, for parametric changes to occur, and for a new informational order to be established. It provides a moment in which informational power in Braman's (2006) sense is renegotiated.

Why does this happen? A state is not only an organizational container to manage power; it is also a moment, a state of organizational existence specifically characterized by its own communicative conditions. The Ukrainian state has experienced several states of being since its independence. The turbulent times in which Ukraine found itself during the Euromaidan events can be seen as a struggle over communicative power as well as a struggle to acquire or appropriate the mandate to exercise that power. The purpose of the struggle to control the management of meaning in Ukraine is not only to support Ukrainians' national identity in the face of outside aggression; ultimately, it is also to form the information dominance that is one of the two powers of the Weberian-Bourdieuan state—that is, a state that has the monopoly of both coercive power and communication power, of both physical violence and symbolic violence. In that sense, the parametric changes related to the Euromaidan events also concern parametric policy, or the power to fundamentally alter who controls how Ukraine should be represented and who should be addressed by these representations. This is not—or at least not only—about which identities are being communicated; it is about the very structural conditions for producing identity *at all*.

One of the tasks the Ministry of Information Policy set out to accomplish was to rebuild the communication infrastructure in the war zones in Donetsk and Luhansk in eastern Ukraine and to restore the ability of mass media—especially television—to operate. Infrastructural technology is, of course, one of the constitutive features for communicating on a national basis. Equally important are how communication is organized and who has the mandate to organize it, irrespective of whether this mandate is given or appropriated. Appropriation, however, cannot be achieved out of the blue. There must be some kind of reference point that legitimizes the speaker's authority to speak in the name of the state. This is why it is so important that nation branding campaigns have at least a small amount of funding from the state budget, as this link to the state administration is constitutive for the mandate and the power to speak in the name of the social whole. A purely commercial campaign funded by private interests would not result in the same authority. Funding must be public for the speaker to legitimately represent the public.

This bond to the state—this authority—must be handled sensitively. The one that speaks for the social whole also must answer to this collective. This is especially important when it comes to representations of national identity, because if the identity represented is not accepted by those in whose name one speaks, there will be criticism. There are countless examples of nation branding campaigns that backfired domestically because the campaigns did not take this consideration seriously and thought mainly about the target group of foreign investors and tourists (see, e.g., Jordan 2014b; Ståhlberg and Bolin 2015). But target audiences are not the ones who mandate someone to speak on their behalf.

The state states, according to Bourdieu; it makes statements. However, it often does so by proxy, through agents over whom it does not have full control. Nonetheless, the state has to appear unified by speaking in a uniform voice, and the media can help construct this voice and this apprehension of a unified center from which the state speaks. In his criticism of Dayan and Katz's (1992) media events theory, Nick Couldry (2003) argues that the media, rather than being a mirror of a coherent and integrated society, construct society through representation as a centralized unity, with a center from which power and authority emanate. According to Couldry, this "myth of the centre" is also a "myth of the mediated centre," by which he means that irrespective of whether a society has a center, the media create the appearance of one and the media act as the chief mediator of that center. This is how the media point to their own importance, by saying there is indeed a power center in society and we, the media, give citizens exclusive access to it. This, Couldry argues, "fulfils a direct institutional purpose: self-justification" (2006, 179). In that sense, the informational state might be diffused, dispersed, and decentralized, speaking from a number of positions and with the voice of multiple agents, but the media would have us believe there is a core that binds all these voices together in a collective "we." In fact, it can be argued that in addition to being technologically constitutive for the informational state by providing the material and distribution infrastructure of messages, the media are also ideologically constitutive through the production of the myth that state authority emanates from one place— the center—and that the media give us access to it.

NARRATIVE CLOSURE: A REVOLUTION FOR THE INFORMATIONAL STATE IN THE TWENTY-FIRST CENTURY?

In the beginning of this book, we accounted for the way Ukraine's post-Soviet sovereignty has been narrated as a gradual change in the Ukrainian state and Ukrainian society through three revolutions: the Revolution on Granite, the Orange Revolution, and the Revolution of Dignity, or the Euromaidan Revolution. Related to how these three revolutions have been described, we might ask what kinds of revolutions they were and what their political and social consequences were. Recall from chapter 1 that we can distinguish between different parameters in transformative processes, and with Colin Sparks (1998) we ask at what level change occurs in the accounts of these revolutionary activities. Were there political changes, and if so, did they occur on a systemic level, or did they consist mainly of an exchange of officials? We have not studied the events as such, so we cannot judge whether they qualify as revolutions. Suffice it to say that it would be hard to see the three occasions as total restructurings of both the political and the social system.

What we have studied is how these events were communicated and constructed in narratives, affective images, discourses, and news snippets spread out over a variety of media platforms. To describe an event as a revolution implies some sort of paradigmatic change of a deep and fundamental kind. Arguably, the Revolution on Granite coincided with Ukraine's independence and could be seen as resulting in such a paradigmatic change. However, it has been characterized as a peaceful student protest, and one could question whether this event is really what overthrew the communist system. It probably makes more sense to regard the students as the illustrative props in the wider story of social and political restructuring. We would rather frame these events as a narrative trope in which the Ukrainian nation-state shook off its Soviet legacy step by step.

The construction of the national history of post-Soviet Ukraine in terms of its three revolutions can thus be said to build on a longer history of narrativization of historical events. One could regard the latter as a story in three acts that reaches narrative closure with the Revolution of Dignity, in the same way *The Battleship Potemkin* reaches narrative closure with the sailors joining forces with the socialist rebels in the final scenes of the film. We learn to understand history and historical development through the stories we tell, but the conditions for storytelling and narrative construction have changed since the days when Sergei Eisenstein was operating. Storytelling has multiplied, involving many more agents and technologies in its production, and it combines textual elements from a much larger paradigm of images, signs, and text fragments. The way Ukraine is presented domestically as well as to others around the world makes this particular story of three revolutions in the twenty-first century a semiotically, organizationally, and technologically complex and interpretatively challenging phenomenon. Whether it will also revolutionize the informational state remains to be seen in future research and analyses.

NOTES

INTRODUCTION

1. The United Nations has declared the Crimean referendum held after the Russian annexation invalid. The occupied territories in Luhansk and Donetsk have not been recognized by the UN either. In this book we regard the Ukrainian borders as those recognized by the UN. Various other sources are less clear on this point.

2. Several new terms have been invented in what could be termed the war and media literature. Hoskins and O'Loughlin (2015) term it "arrested war," while Pötzsch (2013) speaks of "iWar." Hybrid warfare is discussed historically by Murray and Mansoor (2012) and, with special attention to Russia, by Renz (2016). RT has been the object of numerous analyses, among them Miazhevich (2014, 2018), Yablokov (2015), Voronova (2017), and Yablokov and Chatterjee-Doody (2022).

3. Information on the Ukraine Crisis Media Center can be found on its webpage: http://uacrisis.org/about (last accessed 31 October 2019).

4. The economic power of the wealthiest oligarchs has been stable over the years, although their wealth decreased somewhat during the presidency of Petro Poroshenko, who was considered an oligarch himself (Datskevych 2019).

5. In 2014 Transparency International ranked Ukraine 144 out of 177 countries in its Corruption Perception Index (Åslund 2014, 64). In 2021 Ukraine was ranked number 122 (www.transparency.org/en/cpi/2021).

6. For trust in post-Soviet countries, see Bakardjieva et al. (2021, chap. 2).

7. On the concentration of the media market in Ukraine before Euromaidan, see Ryabinska (2011, 11ff.).

8. For details on their various platforms, see Szostek (2014, 3ff.).

9. Thus, we are primarily concerned with the management of meaning in three of the four interrelated frameworks that Ulf Hannerz (1992, 46–52) suggests for analyzing contemporary cultural processes: state, market, and movement. The fourth framework—form of life, referring to everyday consociality and habitual points of view—is only occasionally in focus.

10. "Some advisers, such as Lt. Col. Alexander Vindman, who oversaw Ukraine policy on the National Security Council, told lawmakers that 'outside influencers

were promoting a false narrative of Ukraine' to Trump that was 'harmful to U.S. government policy'" (Jaffe and Dawsey 2019).

CHAPTER 1

1. These phenomena have received substantial attention from political scientists. For an overview of the literature, see Finkel and Brudny (2012a).

2. This was evident after 24 February 2022: When the Russians invaded Ukraine, it immediately became a battle of words as well. While most of the world, including the United Nations, called it an unprovoked invasion and an act of war, Russian authorities term it a "special military operation."

3. A detailed account of agitprop theater in the 1920s and 1930s can be found in Jonsson (2013, 229–241).

4. Already in 1918, Harold Lasswell remarked that it was "bad tactics" by the British to "announce blatantly to the enemy that a 'Director of Propaganda in Enemy Countries' has been named" (1927, 20).

5. For a more detailed discussion of the Chinese version of soft power and how it differs from Western forms, see Repnikova (2022).

6. We have analyzed this campaign (Bolin 2002, 2006a, 2006b, 2010b; Bolin and Ståhlberg 2010), as have others (Jansen 2008, 2012; Jordan 2011, 2014a, 2014b; Polese, Ambrosio, and Kerikmäe 2020). It is often referred to as a historic milestone in analyses of other nation branding campaigns.

7. See Gibbs (2008) on "affect contagion" and Eder (2016) on "affective image operations."

8. The Azov battalion was later incorporated into the National Guard under the Ukrainian Ministry of Interior and thus became part of the regular Ukrainian army. For its early history and discussion of its rather marginal role in the Ukrainian army, see Umland (2019). The Azov battalion received renewed attention in connection to the siege of the Azovstal steel plant in Mariupol during spring 2022.

9. A Google Ngram analysis shows that the concept of strategic narrative started to take off around the turn of the millennium, dramatically rising in popularity shortly before 2010.

10. For an analysis of the ontological differences at the root of the debate between Couldry and Dayan and Katz, see Bolin (2010b, 132ff.).

CHAPTER 2

1. This description was made at a specific point in time, very far from the situation in 2022.

2. For a description and analysis of the operations of RT, see Voronova and Widholm (2019).

3. Ukraine Today was a relatively short-lived project. It stopped broadcasting in 2016 and disappeared from the internet in 2017.

4. Other NGOs engaged in countering negative information about Ukraine include Telekritika, as well as more journalistic NGOs such as Euromaidan Press.

5. In March 2022 Myroshnychenko was appointed Ukraine's ambassador to Australia.

6. Although the website http://prp.com.ua/en/about/services/ is no longer active, it is linked to the PR agency Be-it, run by Natalia Popovych. It states, "We see our mission in creating new meaningful stories that contribute to the development of our country, our market, our team and the businesses of our clients" and "we create the reality, in which we want to live" (be-it.agency, 26 March 2021).

7. See Ukraine Crisis Media Center, "About HWAG," https://uacrisis.org/en /hwag/group.

8. See, for example, these Facebook and Twitter postings: https://www.facebook .com/HybridWarfareAG/?ref=page_internal; https://www.facebook.com/Hybrid WarfareUCMC; https://twitter.com/hwag_ucmc.

9. The joint statement was published on the Ukraine Crisis Media Center's webpage: https://uacrisis.org/en/71966-joint-appeal-of-civil-society-representatives.

CHAPTER 3

1. Mustafa Nayem (2014) downplays his own role to the benefit of the larger movement in one of his accounts of the events.

2. The other dignitaries included the minister of foreign affairs, Leonid Kozhara, and the secretary-general of the World Tourism Organization, Taleb Rifai. The opening panel was moderated by Elena Shapovalova of the State Agency of Ukraine for Tourism and Resorts, and speakers included representatives of the American Chambers of Commerce in Ukraine, the head of the EU delegation in Ukraine, ambassadors from neighboring countries, and representatives from UNESCO.

3. Eurobasket 2015, scheduled to be held in Kyiv since 2011, was quickly relocated to Croatia, France, Germany, and Italy after the violence hit Kyiv in 2013—the first time it was held in more than one country. The 2022 Winter Olympic Games were held in Beijing.

CHAPTER 4

1. By "anthropologists," Dayan and Katz are referring to scholars such as Arnold van Gennep (1909), Claude Lévi-Strauss ([1958] 1977), Victor Turner and Edith Turner (1978), and Anthony Wallace (1966) and their studies of religious ritual sequencing.

2. See also Tetyana Lokot's (2021) account of the meaning of *Europe* in and around the Euromaidan Revolution.

3. The idea that nations need a success story has been widespread in public diplomacy and nation branding discourse internationally (see, e.g., Lepore 2019).

4. For a more detailed discussion of the connection between transformative media events and disruptive events in relation to Euromaidan, see Bolin and Ståhlberg (2022). The concept of disruptive event is developed in Katz and Liebes (2007).

5. An illustrative example is the version sung from the stage on New Year's Eve 2013. Ruslana led the anthem at midnight, together with, among others, Petro Poroshenko, who would eventually be elected president following Yanukovych's escape to Russia. See https://www.youtube.com/watch?v=08-DzumzakY. There are many clips of the singing of the national anthem on YouTube, for example, one from 4 December 2013, at the beginning of the protests: https://www.youtube.com/watch?v=lItPEbc6e-I.

6. For an example from 15 December 2013, see https://www.youtube.com/watch?v=F9EWEB4wru0. Another, more dramatic example, set to the fire of burning tires, is from 18 February 2014: https://www.youtube.com/watch?v=r6ypE3G_pgE. An interesting clip from 9 December 2013 from Radio Svoboda was rebroadcast by Radio Free Europe: https://www.youtube.com/watch?v=-nNFrvGOb9o. Another one was taken from a drone on 16 December 2013: https://www.youtube.com/watch?v=Onk4SDBh6IM.

7. See, for example, CNN, 18 March 2014: https://edition.cnn.com/2014/03/04/world/gallery/irpt-maia-ukraine-essay-duplicate-2/index.html.

8. See, for example, a clip from BBC World, 20 December 2013: https://www.bbc.com/news/world-europe-25468055. For a BBC feature from 10 April 2014, see https://www.youtube.com/watch?v=Wx52GlLTMB8.

9. An excerpt from *Piano* (Drygas 2015) can be seen on YouTube: https://www.youtube.com/watch?v=UEIeXkx3dhE.

10. Thanks to Kateryna Boyko for pointing this out to us.

11. Described in more detail in Bolin (2006b, 195).

12. There is a substantial amount of research on the queer identity politics related to the ESC. See, for example, several contributions in Raykoff and Tobin (2007) and the articles by Baker (2016), Cassiday (2014), and Imre (2020).

13. The Eurovision Song Contest was also held in a location that could be considered in a state at war when Israel hosted the event in 1979, 1999, and 2019 and Russia hosted in 2009 (when it was involved in a war with Georgia).

14. See https://eurovision.tv/about/rules.

15. The air date was 14 May 2016. See https://www.rt.com/viral/343060-eurovision-song-contest-funded.

16. This situation is very similar to what Gregory Bateson, in his writing about schizophrenia, calls the "double bind" (1972, 2008).

17. For a thorough discussion of the EU motto and other EU symbols, such as the musical theme (a compressed version of Ludwig van Beethoven's "Ode to Joy"

from the final movement of his Ninth Symphony), the flag, and the euro, see Johan Fornäs's rich analysis in *Signifying Europe* (2012).

18. See the EU's webpage, https://europa.eu/european-union/about-eu/symbols /motto_en.

19. The fact that Ukraine backed out of the Eurasian Economic Union also cast a shadow on the union's inauguration in May 2014. This was noted internationally, and one of the pieces gained widespread publication (Brooke 2014).

20. The video can be found on YouTube at https://www.youtube.com/watch ?v=KqWhJaYbOa8.

21. The video can be found on YouTube at https://www.youtube.com/watch ?v=KqWhJaYbOa8.

22. The sopilka is a sort of flute, the bandura is a guitar-like instrument, and the buhay is a friction drum.

23. See https://www.radiosvoboda.org/a/news-zbirna-ukrainy-euro-2020-forma /31293132.html. Thanks to Roman Horbyk for helping us research the controversy over the shirt design.

CHAPTER 5

1. This is true not only of journalistic accounts of the events but also of academic writings. It can be traced back to how movements and organizations in Ukrainian nationalism in the twentieth century have been evaluated by historians. Barbara Törnquist-Plewa and Yuliya Yurchuk (2019, 700) helpfully summarize the main academic positions in this debate.

2. We have singled out these authors because they occupy a central position in the field of international relations and are the most referenced sources for definitions of strategic narratives. See also various uses of the concept of narrative in Szostek (2018), Coticchia and Catanzaro (2020), Claessen (2021), Khaldarova (2021), and Wagnsson and Barzanje (2021). Ventsel et al. (2021) combine the theory of strategic narrative with a theoretical discussion based on the cultural semiotics of Lotman, but they resort to a less precise use of the narrative concept. Roberts (2006) writes about "the narrative turn in IR [international relations]," taking his point of departure in "narrative history." Surprisingly—at least to us, having been trained in the narrative theories of Russian formalism and similar forms of narrative sequencing—authors such as Propp and Greimas and the wealth of narrative theory in literature and cinema studies are absent from all these texts.

3. Classic studies include Charlotte Brunsdon and David Morley's (1999) work on the audiences of the British current affairs television program *Nationwide*. Also worth mentioning is Tamar Liebes and Elihu Katz's ([1990] 1993) work on the international reception of the television series *Dallas* in their book *Export of Meaning*. There are, however, numerous audience studies that point to a spectrum of interpretations among viewers, readers, and listeners.

REFERENCES

Alexander, Jeffrey C. 1991. "Habermas and Critical Theory: Beyond the Marxian Dilemma?" In *Communicative Action: Essays on Habermas's Theory of Communicative Action*, edited by Axel Honneth and Hans Joas, 49–73. Cambridge, MA: MIT Press.

Aliyev, Husseyn. 2015. *Post-Communist Civil Society and the Soviet Legacy: Challenges of Democratisation and Reform in the Caucasus*. Houndmills, UK: Palgrave Macmillan.

Andrejevic, Mark. 2007. *iSpy: Surveillance and Power in the Interactive Era*. Lawrence: University Press of Kansas.

Anholt, Simon. 2005. *Brand New Justice: How Branding Places and Products Can Help the Developing World*. Oxford: Elsevier.

Anholt, Simon. 2007. *Competitive Identity: The New Brand Management for Nations, Cities and Regions*. New York: Palgrave Macmillan.

Applebaum, Anne. 2017. *Red Famine: Stalin's War on Ukraine*. London: Allen Lane.

Aronczyk, Melissa. 2007. "New and Improved Nations: Branding National Identity." In *Practicing Culture*, edited by C. Calhoun and R. Sennett, 105–128. London: Routledge.

Aronczyk, Melissa. 2008. "'Living the Brand': Nationality, Globality and the Identity Strategies of Nation Branding Consultants." *International Journal of Communication* 2:41–65.

Aronczyk, Melissa. 2013. *Branding the Nation: The Global Business of National Identity*. Oxford: Oxford University Press.

Åslund, Anders. 2014. "Oligarchs, Corruption, and European Integration." *Journal of Democracy* 25 (3): 64–73.

Austin, John L. (1955) 1975. *How to Do Things with Words: The William James Lectures Delivered at Harvard University in 1955*. Oxford: Clarendon.

Bakardjieva, Maria, Stina Bengtsson, Göran Bolin, and Kjell Engelbrekt. 2021. *Digital Media and the Dynamics of Civil Society: Retooling Citizenship in New EU Democracies*. Lanham, MD: Rowman and Littlefield.

Baker, Catherine. 2016. "The 'Gay Olympics'? The Eurovision Song Contest and the Politics of LGBT/European Belonging." *European Journal of International Relations* 23 (1): 97–121.

Barber, Lynsay. 2014. "Ukraine Challenges Russian Media with Launch of International News Channel Ukraine Today." *City A.M.*, 21 July. https://www.cityam.com/?s=Ukraine+Challenges+Russian+Media+with+Launch+of+International+News+Channel+Ukraine+Today.

Barthes, Roland. (1964) 1977. "The Rhetoric of the Image." In *Image—Music—Text*, 32–51. London: Fontana.

Barthes, Roland. (1966) 1977. "Introduction to the Structural Analysis of Narratives." In *Image—Music—Text*, 79–124. London: Fontana.

Barthes, Roland. (1968) 1977. "The Death of the Author." In *Image—Music—Text*, 142–148. London: Fontana.

Bateson, Gregory. 1972. *Steps to an Ecology of Mind: Collected Essays in Anthropology, Psychiatry, Evolution, and Epistemology*. Part III. *Form and Pathology in Relationship*. San Francisco: Chandler.

BBC News. 2014. "Profile: Ukraine's Ultra-nationalist Right Sector." 28 April. https://www.bbc.com/news/world-europe-27173857.

BBC News. 2017. "Eurovision in Ukraine: Controversy over Russian Entry." 13 March. https://www.bbc.com/news/world-europe-39254404.

Bernays, Edward. (1928) 2005. *Propaganda*. New York: IG Publishing.

Bezpiatchuk, Zhanna. 2011. "Branding Ukraine: Lip-synching a Happy Tune." *Ukrainian Week*, 20 December. http://ukrainianweek.com/Society/38090.

Boli, John, and George M. Thomas. 1999. *Constructing World Culture: International Nongovernmental Organizations since 1875*. Stanford, CA: Stanford University Press.

Bolin, Göran. 2002. "Nationsmarknadsföring. Eurovisionsschlagerfestivalen som modern världsutställning." In *Hello Europe! Tallinn Calling! Eurovision Song Contest 2002 som mediehändelse*, edited by Staffan Ericson, 33–42. Huddinge, Sweden: Södertörn University.

Bolin, Göran. 2003. *Variations, Media Landscapes, History: Frameworks for an Analysis of Contemporary Media Landscapes*. Huddinge, Sweden: Södertörn University.

Bolin, Göran. 2006a. "Electronic Geographies: Media Landscapes as Technological and Symbolic Environments." In *Geographies of Communication: The Spatial Turn in Media Studies*, edited by Jesper Falkheimer and André Jansson, 67–86. Göteborg, Sweden: Nordicom.

Bolin, Göran. 2006b. "Visions of Europe: Cultural Technologies of Nation-states." *International Journal of Cultural Studies* 9 (2): 189–206.

Bolin, Göran. 2009. "Television Textuality: Textual Forms in Live Television Programming." *Nordicom Review* 30 (1): 37–53.

Bolin, Göran. 2010a. "Digitization, Multi-Platform Texts and Audience Reception." *Popular Communication* 8 (1): 72–83.

Bolin, Göran. 2010b. "Media Events, Eurovision and Societal Centers." In *Media Events in a Global Age*, edited by Nick Couldry, Andreas Hepp, and Friedrich Krotz, 124–138. London: Routledge.

Bolin, Göran. 2014. "Television Journalism, Politics and Entertainment: Power and Autonomy in the Field of Television Journalism." *Television and New Media* 15 (4): 336–349.

Bolin, Göran. 2016. "Afterword: The Construction of a Market for Place Branding and Public Diplomacy—A View from the North." *Place Branding and Public Diplomacy* 12 (2): 236–241.

Bolin, Göran. 2017. *Media Generations: Experience, Identity and Mediatised Social Change*. London: Routledge.

Bolin, Göran, Paul Jordan, and Per Ståhlberg. 2016. "From Nation Branding to Information Warfare: Management of Information in the Ukraine–Russia Conflict." In *Media and the Ukraine Crisis: Hybrid Media Practices and Narratives of Conflict*, edited by Mervi Pantti, 3–18. New York: Peter Lang.

Bolin, Göran, and Galina Miazhevich. 2018. "The Soft Power of Commercialized Nationalist Symbols: Using Media Analysis to Understand Nation Branding Campaigns." *European Journal of Cultural Studies* 21 (5): 527–542.

Bolin, Göran, and Per Ståhlberg. 2010. "Between Community and Commodity: Nationalism and Nation Branding." In *Communicating the Nation: National Topographies of Global Media Landscapes*, edited by Anna Roosvall and Inka Salovaara Moring, 79–101. Göteborg, Sweden: Nordicom.

Bolin, Göran, and Per Ståhlberg. 2015. "Mediating the Nation-state: Agency and the Media in Nation-Branding Campaigns." *International Journal of Communication* 9:3065–3083.

Bolin, Göran, and Per Ståhlberg. 2021. "The Powerpoint Nation: Branding an Imagined Commodity." *European Review* 29 (4): 445–456.

Bolin, Göran, and Per Ståhlberg. 2022. "Disruption and Transformation in Media Events Theory: The Case of the Euromaidan Revolution in Ukraine." *Nordic Journal of Media Studies* 4:99–117.

Bolter, Jay David, and Richard Grusin. 2000. *Remediation: Understanding New Media*. Cambridge, MA: MIT Press.

Bourdieu, Pierre. (1983) 1986. "The Forms of Capital." In *Handbook of Theory and Research for the Sociology of Education*, edited by John G. Richardson, 241–258. New York: Greenwood Press.

Bourdieu, Pierre. 1990. *In Other Words: Essays towards a Reflexive Sociology*. Cambridge: Polity.

Bourdieu, Pierre. 1991. *Language and Symbolic Power*. Cambridge: Polity.

Bourdieu, Pierre. 1996. *The State Nobility: Elite Schools in the Field of Power*. Cambridge: Polity.

Bourdieu, Pierre. (2012) 2020. *On the State: Lectures at the Collège de France 1989–1992*. Cambridge: Polity.

Braman, Sandra. 2006. *Change of State: Information, Policy, and Power*. Cambridge, MA: MIT Press.

Braman, Sandra. 2019. "Trumpean Nation Branding: Strange Attractions and Information Policy." In *Fritt från fältet: Om medier, generationer och värden—Festskrift till Göran Bolin*, edited by Peter Jakobsson and Fredrik Stiernstedt, 149–167. Huddinge, Sweden: Södertörn University.

Braman, Sandra. 2021. "Ecstacy and Entropy: Information Policy in a Punctuated Case." In *Research Handbook in Information Policy*, edited by Alistair Duff, 40–55. Cheltenham, UK: Edward Elgar Publishing.

Brooke, James. 2014. "Putin Kicks off Eurasian Union, without Ukraine." Voice of America, 29 May. https://www.voanews.com/a/russia-belarus-kazakhstan-agree-to-create-economic-union/1924941.html.

Bruns, Axel. 2006. "Towards Produsage: Futures for User-Led Content Production." In *Proceedings: Cultural Attitudes towards Communication and Technology 2006*, edited by Fay Sudweeks, Herbert Hrachovec, and Charles Ess, 275–284. Perth, Australia: Murdoch University.

Brunsdon, Charlotte, and David Morley. 1999. *The Nationwide Television Studies*. London: Routledge.

Burke, Kenneth. 1969. *A Rhetoric of Motives*. Berkeley: University of California Press.

Business Ukraine. 2015. "Ukraine's Infowar Amazon: Minister Tetyana Popova Seeks to Make Ukrainian Army Media-Savvy." 19 June. http://bunews.com.ua/politics/item/ukraine-s-infowar-amazon-deputy-minister-for-information-policy-tetyana-popova-seeks-to-make-ukrainian-army-media-savvy.

Carey, James, ed. 1983. *Media, Myths and Narratives: Television and the Press*. Newbury Park, CA: Sage.

Carlón, Mario. 2020a. "Between the Power of Enunciators and the Power of Discourses: The Hypermedia Circulation of Contemporary Images." In *Networks, Societies, and Polis: Epistemological Approaches on Mediatization*, edited by Jairo Ferreira, Pedro Gilberto Gomes, Antonio Fausto Neto, José Luiz Braga, and Ana Paula da Rosa, 215–236. Santa Maria, Brazil: FACOS–UFSM.

Carlón, Mario. 2020b. *Circulation del sentido y construccion de colectivos en una sociedad hipermediatizada*. San Luis, Argentina: Nueva Editorial Universitaria.

Cassiday, Julie A. 2014. "Post-Soviet Pop Goes Gay: Russia's Trajectory to Eurovision Victory." *Russian Review* 73 (1): 1–23.

Castells, Manuel. 2009. *Communication Power*. Oxford: Oxford University Press.

Choo, Chun Wei. 2006. *The Knowing Organization: How Organizations Use Information to Construct Meaning, Create Knowledge, and Make Decisions*. New York: Oxford University Press.

Chraibi, Christine. 2016. "A Short History of the Ukrainian Greeting 'Slava Ukrayini.'" Euromaidan Press, 13 June. http://euromaidanpress.com/2016/06/13/a-short-history-of-the-ukrainian-greeting-slava-ukrayini/.

Ciechalski, Suzanne, Caitlin Fichtel, and Rima Abdelkader. 2020. "New Video Appears to Show George Floyd on the Ground with Three Officers." *NBC News*, 29 May. https://www.nbcnews.com/news/us-news/new-video-appears-show-george-floyd-ground-three-officers-n1217476.

Claessen, Eva. 2021. "The Making of a Narrative: The Use of Geopolitical Othering in Russian Strategic Narratives during the Ukraine Crisis." *Media, War & Conflict*. https://doi.org/10.1177/17506352211029529.

Corrigan, Philip, and Derek Sayer. 1985. *The Great Arch: English State Formation as Cultural Revolution*. Oxford: Blackwell.

Coticchia, Fabrizio, and Andrea Catanzaro. 2020. "The Fog of Words: Assessing the Problematic Relationship between Strategic Narratives." *Media, War & Conflict*. https://doi.org/10.1177/1750635220965622.

Couldry, Nick. 2000. *The Place of Media Power: Pilgrims and Witnesses of the Media Age*. London: Routledge.

Couldry, Nick. 2003. *Media Rituals: A Critical Approach*. London: Routledge.

Couldry, Nick. 2006. "Transvaluing Media Studies, or, Beyond the Myth of the Mediated Centre." In *Media and Cultural Theory*, edited by James Curran and David Morley, 177–194. London: Routledge.

Couldry, Nick. 2016. "Life with the Media Manifold: Between Freedom and Subjection." In *Politics, Civil Society and Participation: Media and Communications in a Transforming Environment*, edited by Leif Kramp, Nico Carpentier, Andreas Hepp, Richard Kilborn, Risto Kunelius, Hannu Nieminen, Tobias Olsson, Pille Pruulmann-Vengerfeldt, Ilija Tomanić Trivundža, and Simone Tosoni, 25–40. Bremen, Germany: Edition lumière.

Couldry, Nick, Andreas Hepp, and Friedrich Krotz. 2010. *Media Events in a Global Age*. London: Routledge.

Crichton, Michael. 1993. "Mediasaurus." *Wired*, 1 April. www.wired.com/1993/04/mediasaurus/.

Cull, Nicholas J. 2019. *Public Diplomacy: Foundations for Global Engagement in the Digital Age*. Cambridge: Polity Press.

Dahlgren, Peter. 1999. "Television News Narrative." In *Framing Friction: Media and Social Conflict*, edited by Mary S. Mander, 189–214. Champaign: University of Illinois Press.

Das Ranjana, Jelena Kleut, and Göran Bolin. 2013. "New Genres—New Roles for the Audience? An Overview of Recent Research." In *Audience Transformations: Shifting Audience Positions in Late Modernity*, edited by Nico Carpentier, Kim Christian Schröder, and Laurie Hallett, 30–46. London: Routledge.

Datskevych, Natalia. 2019. "New Ranking, Same Oligarchs: Meet Ukraine's Richest People." *Kyiv Post*, 31 October. https://www.kyivpost.com/business/new -ranking-same-oligarchs-meet-ukraines-richest-people.html.

Davenport, Thomas H., and John C. Beck. 2001. *The Attention Economy: Understanding the New Currency of Business*. Boston: Harvard Business Press.

Dayan, Daniel, and Elihu Katz. 1992. *Media Events: The Live Broadcasting of History*. Cambridge, MA: Harvard University Press.

Delanty, Gerard, Liana Giorgi, and Monica Sassatelli. 2011. *Festivals and the Cultural Public Sphere*. Abingdon, UK: Routledge.

Detlor, Brian. 2010. "Information Management." *International Journal of Information Management* 30 (2): 103–108.

Dewey, John. 1916. *Democracy and Education: An Introduction to the Philosophy of Education*. New York: Macmillan.

Dinnie, Ketth. 2008. *Nation Branding: Concepts, Issues, Practice*. Oxford: Butterworth-Heinemann.

Drotner, Kirsten. 1994. "Ethnographic Enigmas: 'The Everyday' in Recent Media Studies." *Cultural Studies* 8 (2): 341–357.

Drygas, Vita Maria. 2015. *Piano*. TV documentary. Drygas Production.

Dyczok, Marta. 2014. "Information Wars: Hegemony, Counter-Hegemony, Propaganda, the Use of Force, and Resistance." *Russian Journal of Communication* 6 (2): 173–176.

Dyczok, Marta. 2016. *Ukraine's Euromaidan: Broadcasting through Information Wars with Hromadske Radio*. Bristol, UK: E–International Relations Publishing.

Eco, Umberto. (1980) 1994. *The Name of the Rose*. San Diego: Harcourt Brace.

Eco, Umberto. 1981. "Narrative Structures in Fleming." In *The Role of the Reader*, 144–172. London: Hutchinson.

Eder, Jens. 2016. "Affective Image Operations." In *Image Operations: Visual Media and Political Conflict*, edited by Jens Eder and Charlotte Klonk, 63–78. Manchester, UK: Manchester University Press.

Eisenstein, Sergei. (1949) 1977. *Film Form: Essays in Film Theory*. New York: Harcourt, Brace and World.

Ellis, John. 1992. *Visible Fictions: Cinema, Television, Video*. 2nd ed. London: Routledge.

Ellis, John. 2000. *Seeing Things: Television in the Age of Uncertainty*. London: I. B. Tauris.

Ellul, Jacques. 1965. *Propaganda: The Formation of Men's Attitudes*. New York: Alfred A. Knopf.

Entman, Robert M. 2008. "Theorizing Mediated Diplomacy: The US Case." *International Journal of Press/Politics* 13 (2): 87–102.

Ericson, Staffan. 2002. "Rösten från andra sidan: En kommentar till kommentaren." In *Hello Europe! Tallinn Calling! Eurovisionsschlagerfestivalen som mediehändelse*, edited by Staffan Ericson, 43–68. Huddinge, Sweden: Södertörn University.

Farkas, Johan, and Jannick Schou. 2020. *Post-Truth, Fake News and Democracy: Mapping the Politics of Falsehood*. London: Routledge.

Fedirko, Taras. 2021. "Liberalism in Fragments: Oligarchy and the Liberal Subject in Ukrainian News Journalism." *Social Anthropology/Anthropologie Sociale* 29 (2): 471–489.

Finkel, Evgeny, and Yitzhak M. Brudny. 2012a. No More Colour! Authoritarian Regimes and Colour Revolutions in Eurasia." *Democratization* 19 (1): 1–14.

Finkel, Evgeny, and Yitzhak M. Brudny. 2012b. "Russia and the Colour Revolutions." *Democratization* 19 (1): 15–36.

Fiske, John. 1994. *Media Matters: Everyday Culture and Political Change*. New York: Routledge.

Fornäs, Johan. 2012. *Signifying Europe*. Bristol, UK: Intellect.

Fornäs, Johan. 2017. "Europe Faces Europe: An Introduction." In *Europe Faces Europe: Narratives from Its Eastern Half*, edited by Johan Fornäs, 1–34. Bristol, UK: Intellect.

Foucault, Michel. 2007. *Security, Territory, Population: Lectures at Collège de France, 1977–78*. New York: Palgrave Macmillan.

Furhammar, Leif, and Folke Isaksson. 1968. *Politik och film*. Stockholm: PAN/Norstedts.

Geertz, Clifford. 1973. *The Interpretation of Cultures*. New York: Basic Books.

Genette, Gerard. 1997. *Paratexts: Thresholds of Interpretation*. Cambridge: Cambridge University Press.

Gerbner, George. 2010. "Telling All the Stories: Children and Television." *Sacred Heart University Review* 16 (1): 37–54. http://digitalcommons.sacredheart.edu/shureview/vol16/iss1/2.

Gerdes, Stefanie. 2017. "Kiev Gets World's Biggest Rainbow to Promote Diversity." *Gay Star News*, 26 April. https://www.gaystarnews.com/article/kiev-worlds-biggest-rainbow/.

Gibbons-Neff, Thomas. 2015. "At Point 18 in Eastern Ukraine, the War Grinds on, Night after Night." *Washington Post*, 15 August. https://www.washingtonpost.com/world/national-security/at-point-18-in-eastern-ukraine-the-war-grinds-on-night-after-night/2015/08/15/fffcf2c0-405f-11e5-9561-4b3dc93e3b9a_story.html.

Gibbs, Anna. 2008. "Panic! Affect Contagion, Mimesis and Suggestion in the Social Field." *Cultural Studies Review* 14 (2): 130–145.

Glander, Timothy. 2000. *Origins of Mass Communications Research during the American Cold War: Educational Effects and Contemporary Implications.* Mahwah, NJ: Lawrence Erlbaum.

Goffman, Erving. (1974) 1986. *Frame Analysis: An Essay on the Organization of Experience.* Boston: Northeastern University Press.

Goldman, Robert. 1992. *Reading Ads Socially.* London: Routledge.

Graan, Andrew. 2013. "Counterfeiting the Nation? Skopje 2014 and the Politics of Nation Branding in Macedonia." *Cultural Anthropology* 28 (1): 161–179.

Gray, Jonathan. 2010. *Show Sold Separately: Promos, Spoilers, and Other Media Paratexts.* New York: New York University Press.

Grytsenko, Oksana. 2014. "Journalists, Free Speech Activists Protest against 'Ministry of Truth.'" *Kyiv Post,* 4 December. https://www.kyivpost.com/article /content/reform-watch/journalists-media-rights-activists-demand-abolishing-of-new ly-formed-ministry-of-truth-374003.html.

Gupta, Akhil. 2012. *Red Tape: Bureaucracy, Structural Violence, and Poverty in India.* Durham, NC: Duke University Press.

Habermas, Jürgen. (1976) 1979. "What Is Universal Pragmatics?" In *Communication and the Evolution of Society,* 1–68. Boston: Beacon Press.

Habermas, Jürgen. (1981) 1991. *The Theory of Communicative Action.* Vol. 1. *Reason and the Rationalization of Society.* Cambridge: Polity.

Habermas, Jürgen. (1981) 1992. *The Theory of Communicative Action.* Vol. 2. *The Critique of Functionalist Reason.* Cambridge: Polity.

Hall, Jamieson K. 2019. *Cyber War: How Russian Hackers and Trolls Helped Elect a President.* Oxford: Oxford University Press.

Hall, Stuart. 1973. "Encoding/Decoding in the Television Discourse." CCCS Occasional Paper 7. Birmingham University/CCCS, Birmingham, UK.

Hannerz, Ulf. 1992. *Cultural Complexity: Studies in the Social Organization of Meaning.* New York: Columbia University Press.

Hannerz, Ulf. 2004. *Foreign News: Exploring the World of Foreign Correspondents.* Chicago: University of Chicago Press.

Hannerz, Ulf. 2016. *Writing Future Worlds: An Anthropologist Explores Global Scenarios.* London: Palgrave Macmillan.

Hardtmann, Eva-Maria. 2009. *The Dalit Movement in India: Local Practices, Global Connections.* New Delhi: Oxford University Press.

Hazan, Haim, and Ester Hertzog, eds. 2011. *Serendipity in Anthropological Research: The Nomadic Turn.* Farnham, UK: Ashgate.

Heftberger, Adelheid. 2015. "Propaganda in Motion: Dziga Vertov, Aleksandr Medvedkin, Soviet Agitation on Agit-trains, Agit-steamers, and the Film Train in the 1920s and 1930s." *Apparatus: Film, Media and Digital Cultures in Central and Eastern Europe* 1. https://www.apparatusjournal.net/index.php/apparatus/article/view/2.

Herman, Edward S., and Noam Chomsky. 1988. *Manufacturing Consent: The Political Economy of the Mass Media*. New York: Pantheon Books.

Horbyk, Roman. 2017. "Mediated Europes: Discourse and Power in Ukraine, Russia and Poland during Euromaidan." Dissertation, Södertörn University.

Horbyk, Roman. 2019. "In Pursuit of Kairos: Ukrainian Journalists between Agency and Structure during Euromaidan." *Baltic Worlds* 12 (1): 4–19.

Horbyk, Roman, Isabel Löfgren, Yana Prymachenko, and Cheryll Soriano. 2021. "Fake News as Meta-Mimesis: Imitative Genres and Storytelling in the Philippines, Brazil, Russia and Ukraine." *Popular Inquiry* 2021 (1): 30–54.

Hoskins, Andrew, and Ben O'Loughlin. 2015. "Arrested War: The Third Phase of Mediatization." *Information, Communication & Society* 18 (11): 1320–1338.

Hromadske TV. 2016. "Information Ministry Official Resigns over Mistreatment of Journalists." 5 August. https://www.youtube.com/watch?v=WrkCVxuxwcs.

Imre, Anikó. 2020. "The Eurovision Song Contest: Queer Nationalism." In *How to Watch Television*, 2nd ed., edited by Ethan Thompson and Jason Mittell, 193–202. New York: New York University Press.

Interfax Ukraine. 2014. "Poroshenko: Information Ministry's Main Task Is to Repel Information Attacks against Ukraine." 8 December. https://en.interfax.com.ua/news/economic/238615.html.

Interfax Ukraine. 2016. "Jamala Becomes Honored Artist of Ukraine." 16 May. https://en.interfax.com.ua/news/general/343707.html.

Iser, Wolfgang. 1974. *The Implied Reader: Patterns of Communication in Prose Fiction from Bunyan to Beckett*. Baltimore: Johns Hopkins University Press.

Ishchenko, Volodomyr. 2016. "Far Right Participation in the Ukrainian Maidan Protests: An Attempt of Systematic Estimation." *European Politics and Society* 17 (4): 453–472.

Jaffe, Greg, and Josh Dawsey. 2019. "A Presidential Loathing for Ukraine Is at the Heart of the Impeachment Inquiry." *Washington Post*, 2 November. https://www.washingtonpost.com/national-security/a-presidential-loathing-for-ukraine-is-at-the-heart-of-the-impeachment-inquiry/2019/11/02/8280ee60-fcc5-11e9-ac8c-8eced29ca6ef_story.html.

Jansen, Sue Curry. 2008. "Designer Nations: Neo-liberal Nation Branding—Brand Estonia." *Social Identities* 14 (1): 121–142.

Jansen, Sue Curry. 2012. "Redesigning a Nation: Welcome to E-stonia, 2001–2018." In *Branding Post-Communist Nations: Marketizing National Identities in the "New" Europe*, edited by Natalia Kaneva, 79–98. New York: Routledge.

Jenkins, Henry, Sam Ford, and Joshua Green. 2013. *Spreadable Media: Creating Value and Meaning in a Networked Culture*. New York: New York University Press.

Jonsson, Stefan. 2013. *Crowds and Democracy: The Idea and Image of the Masses from Revolution to Fascism*. New York: Columbia University Press.

Jordan, Paul. 2011. "The Eurovision Song Contest: Nation Branding and Nation Building in Estonia and Ukraine." PhD thesis, University of Glasgow.

Jordan, Paul. 2014a. *The Modern Fairy Tale: Nation Branding, National Identity and the Eurovision Song Contest in Estonia*. Tartu, Estonia: Tartu University Press.

Jordan, Paul. 2014b. "Nation Branding: A Tool for Nationalism?" *Journal of Baltic Studies* 45 (3): 283–303.

Jordan, Paul. 2015. "From Ruslana to Gaitana: Performing 'Ukrainianness' in the Eurovision Song Contest." *Contemporary Southeastern Europe* 2 (1): 110–135.

Jowett, Garth S., and Victoria O'Donnell. 1992. *Propaganda and Persuasion*. 2nd ed. Newbury Park, CA: Sage.

Junes, Tom. 2016. "Euromaidan and the Revolution of Dignity: A Case Study of Student Protest as a Catalyst for Political Upheaval." *Critique & Humanism* 46 (2): 73–96.

Kabachiy, Roman. 2013. "Backwood Viewpoint." *Kyiv Weekly* 18:2–3.

Kaneva, Nadia. 2011. "Nation Branding: Toward an Agenda for Critical Research." *International Journal of Communication* 5:117–141.

Kaneva, Nadia, ed. 2012. *Branding Post-Communist Nations: Marketizing National Identities in the "New" Europe*. New York: Routledge.

Kaneva, Nadia. 2018. "Simulation Nations: Nation Brands and Baudrillard's Theory of Media." *European Journal of Cultural Studies* 21 (5): 631–648.

Kaneva, Nadia, and D. Popescu. 2011. "National Identity Lite: Nation Branding in Post-Communist Romania and Bulgaria." *International Journal of Cultural Studies* 14 (2): 191–207.

Kasianov, Georgiy. 2022. "Holodomor and the Holocaust in Ukraine as Cultural Memory: Comparison, Competition, Interaction." *Journal of Genocide Research* 24 (2): 216–227.

Katz, Elihu, and Paul F. Lazarsfeld. 1955. *Personal Influence: The Part Played by the People in the Flow of Mass Communications*. Glencoe, IL: Free Press.

Katz, Elihu, and Tamar Liebes. 2007. "'No More Peace!' How Disaster, Terror and War Has Upstaged Media Events." *International Journal of Communication* 1:157–166.

Kenez, P. 1985. *The Birth of the Propaganda State: Soviet Methods of Mass Mobilization, 1917–1929*. Cambridge: Cambridge University Press.

Kernbach, Sebastian, Sabrina Bresciani, and Martin J. Eppler. 2015. "Slip-Sliding Away: A Review of the Literature on the Constraining Qualities of PowerPoint." *Business and Professional Communication Quarterly* 78 (3): 292–313.

Khaldarova, Irina. 2021. "Brother or 'Other'? Transformation of Strategic Narratives in Russian Television News during the Ukraine Crisis." *Media, War & Conflict* 14 (1): 3–20.

Kjeldsen, Jens E. 2006. "The Rhetoric of PowerPoint." *International Journal of Media, Technology and Lifelong Learning* 2:1–17.

Knoblauch, Hubert. 2008. "The Performance of Knowledge: Pointing and Knowledge in PowerPoint Presentations." *Cultural Sociology* 2 (1): 75–97.

Kølvraa, Christoffer. 2015. "Affect, Provocation, and Far Right Rhetoric." In *Affective Methodologies: Developing Cultural Research Strategies for the Study of Affect*, edited by B. T. Knudsen and C. Stage, 183–200. London: Palgrave.

Kremer, Arkady, and Yuli Martov. (1896) 1983. "On Agitation." In *Marxism in Russia: Key Documents 1879–1906*, edited by Neil Harding, 192–205. Cambridge: Cambridge University Press.

Kuzio, Taras. 2017. *Putin's War against Ukraine: Revolution, Nationalism, and Crime.* Toronto: University of Toronto.

Kyriakidou, Maria, Michael Skey, Julie Uldam, and Patrick McCurdy. 2018. "Media Events and Cosmopolitan Fandom: 'Playful Nationalism' in the Eurovision Song Contest." *International Journal of Cultural Studies* 21 (6): 603–618.

Laar, Mart. 1996. "Estonia's Success Story." *Journal of Democracy* 7 (1): 96–101.

Langley, Alison. 2014. "Ukraine Today Aims to Clarify Russian Media Misinformation." *Columbia Journalism Review*, 27 August. http://www.cjr.org/behind_the_news/ukraine_today_russian_media.php.

Lasswell, Harold D. 1927. "The Theory of Political Propaganda." *American Political Science Review* 21 (3): 627–631.

Lasswell, Harold D. (1927) 1971. *Propaganda Technique in World War I.* Cambridge, MA: MIT Press.

Lasswell, Harold D. 1941. *Democracy through Public Opinion.* Menasha, WI: Georg Banta.

Lasswell, Harold D. 1948. "The Structure and Function of Communication in Society." In *The Communication of Ideas*, edited by Lyman Bryson, 37–51. New York: Harper and Row.

Lasswell, Harold D., and Dorothy Blumenstock. 1939. *World Revolutionary Propaganda: A Chicago Study.* New York: A. A. Knopf.

Lazarsfeld, Paul F. 1941. "Remarks on Administrative and Critical Communications Research." *Studies in Philosophy and Social Science* 9 (1): 2–16.

Le Bon, Gustave. (1896) 1912. *Massans psykologi.* Stockholm: Bonnier.

Le Bon, Gustave. (1896) 2006. *The Crowd: A Study of the Popular Mind.* New York: Cosimo Classics.

le Carré, John. 1963. *The Spy Who Came in from the Cold*. London: Gollancz.

Lepore, Jill. 2019. "The New Americanism: Why a Nation Needs a National Story." *Foreign Affairs*, March–April. https://www.foreignaffairs.com/articles/united-states /2019-02-05/new-americanism-nationalism-jill-lepore?check_logged_in=1.

Lévi-Strauss, Claude. (1958) 1977. *Structural Anthropology*. Harmondsworth, UK: Penguin Books.

Liebes, Tamar, and Elihu Katz. (1990) 1993. *The Export of Meaning: Cross-cultural Readings of* Dallas. Cambridge: Polity Press.

Likhachev, Vyacheslav. 2014. "Pravyi sektor i drugie." *Forum noveishei vostochnoev-ropeiskoi istorii i kultury*, Russian edition, 11 (2): 75–116.

Lippmann, Walter. (1922) 1946. *Public Opinion*. New York: Penguin.

Lokot, Tetyana. 2021. "Ukraine Is Europe? Complicating the Concept of the 'European' in the Wake of an Urban Protest." *Communication and Critical/Cultural Studies* 18 (4): 439–446.

Lotman, Juri. (1984) 2005. "On the Semiosphere." *Sign Systems Studies* 33 (1): 205–229.

Lury, Celia. 2012. "Going Live: Towards an Amphibious Sociology." *Sociological Review* 60 (1 suppl): 184–197.

Madianou, Mirca, and Daniel Miller. 2011. *Migration and New Media: Transnational Families and Polymedia*. New York: Routledge.

Magocsi, Paul Robert. 2010. *A History of Ukraine: The Land and Its Peoples*. 2nd rev. and expanded ed. Toronto: Toronto University Press.

Manning, Chelsea. 2014. "The Fog Machine of War." *New York Times*, 14 June. https://www.nytimes.com/2014/06/15/opinion/sunday/chelsea-manning-the-us -militarys-campaign-against-media-freedom.html.

Marx, Karl. (1867) 1976. *Capital: A Critique of Political Economy*. Vol. 1. London: Penguin Books.

McCombs, Maxwell E., and Donald L. Shaw. 1972. "The Agenda-setting Function of Mass Media." *Public Opinion Quarterly* 36 (2): 176–187.

Melissen, Jan, ed. 2005. *The New Public Diplomacy: Soft Power in International Relations*. Houndmills, UK: Palgrave Macmillan.

Merton, Robert K. 1948. "The Bearing of Empirical Research upon the Development of Social Theory." *American Sociological Review* 13 (5): 505–515.

Merton, Robert K. (1949) 1957. *Social Theory and Social Structure*. Glencoe, IL: Free Press/Collier-Macmillan.

Merton, Robert K. 1995. "The Thomas Theorem and the Metthew Effect." *Social Forces* 74 (2): 379–424.

Metzger, Meghan MacDuffee, and Joshua A. Tucker. 2017. "Social Media and EuroMaidan: A Review Essay." *Slavic Review* 76 (1): 169–191.

Meyer, John W., John Boli, George M. Thomas, and Francisco O. Ramirez. 1997. "World Society and the Nation-state." *American Journal of Sociology* 103 (1): 144–181.

Miazhevich, Galina. 2014. "*Russia Today*'s Coverage of Euromaidan." *Russian Journal of Communication* 6 (2): 186–191.

Miazhevich, Galina. 2018. "Nation Branding in the Post-Broadcast Era: The Case of RT." *European Journal of Cultural Studies* 21 (5): 575–593.

Mihelj, Sabina, and Simon Huxtable. 2018. *From Media Systems to Media Cultures: Understanding Socialist Television.* Cambridge: Cambridge University Press.

Mikos, Lothar. 2010. "Films, TV Shows, YouTube and the Creativity of Fan Communities." Paper presented at the 60th annual ICA conference, Singapore, 22–26 June.

Miskimmon, Alister, Ben O'Loughlin, and Laura Roselle. 2013. *Strategic Narratives: Communication Power and the New World Order.* New York: Routledge.

Moldovan, Ioana. 2015. "What It's Like on the Front Lines of the War in Ukraine." *Huffington Post*, 2 September. https://www.huffpost.com/entry/ukraine-war-front-lines-photos_b_8079828?utm_hp_ref=world.

Münsterberg, Hugo. 1916. *The Photoplay: A Psychological Study.* New York: D. Appleton.

Murray, Williamson, and Peter R. Mansoor. 2012. *Hybrid Warfare: Fighting Complex Opponents from the Ancient World to the Present.* New York: Cambridge University Press.

Nayem, Mustafa. 2014. "Uprising in Ukraine: How It All Began." *Voices*, 4 April. https://www.opensocietyfoundations.org/voices/uprising-ukraine-how-it-all-began.

Novick, Rebecca. 2014. "The Piano Extremist: Maestro of Euromaidan." *Huffpost*, 14 February. https://www.huffpost.com/entry/the-piano-extremist-maest_b_4834523.

Nye, Joseph. 2004. *Soft Power.* New York: Public Affairs.

Nye, Joseph. 2010. "The Future of Soft Power in US Foreign Policy." In *Soft Power and US Foreign Policy: Theoretical, Historical and Contemporary Perspectives*, edited by Inderjeet Parmar and Michael Cox, 4–11. London: Routledge.

Nye, Joseph S. 2008. "Public Diplomacy and Soft Power." *Annals of the American Academy of Political and Social Science* 616 (1): 94–109.

Nye, Joseph S. 2014. "The Information Revolution and Soft Power." *Current History* 113 (759): 19–22.

Oliinyk, Anna, and Taraz Kuzio. 2021. "The Euromaidan Revolution, Reforms and Decommunisation in Ukraine." *Europe-Asia Studies* 73 (5): 807–836.

Olins, Wally. 2002. "Branding the Nation—The Historical Context." *Journal of Brand Management* 9 (4–5): 241–248.

Onuch, Olga. 2015a. "'Facebook Helped Me Do It': Understanding the Euro-Maidan Protestor 'Tool-kit.'" *Studies in Ethnicity and Nationalism* 15 (1): 170–184.

Onuch, Olga. 2015b. "Maidans Past and Present: Comparing the Orange Revolution and the EuroMaidan." In *Ukraine's Euromaidan: Analysis of a Civil Revolution*, edited by David R. Marples and Frederick V. Mills, 27–56. New York: Columbia University Press.

Orlova, Dariya. 2016. "EuroMaidan: Mediated Protests, Rituals and Nation-in-the-Making." In *Media Events: A Critical Contemporary Approach*, edited by Bianca Mitu and Stamatis Poulakidakos, 207–229. Houndmills, UK: Palgrave Macmillan.

Pamment, James. 2013. *New Public Diplomacy in the 21st Century: A Comparative Study of Policy and Practice*. London: Routledge.

Pieke, Frank. 2000. "Serendipity: Reflections on Fieldwork in China." In *Anthropologists in a Wider World: Essays on Field Research*, edited by Paul Dresch, Wendy James, and David Parkin, 129–150. New York: Berghahn Books.

Pike, Steven Louis. 2021. "The 'American Century' Is Over: The US Global Leadership Narrative, Uncertainty and Public Diplomacy." In *Public Diplomacy and the Politics of Uncertainty*, edited by Pawel Surowiec and Ilan Manor, 3–28. Cham, Switzerland: Palgrave Macmillan.

Pikulicka-Wilczewska, Agnieszka, and Richard Sakwa. 2015. *Ukraine and Russia: People, Politics, Propaganda and Perspectives*. Bristol, UK: E–International Relations Publishing.

Plekhanov, Georgi V. (1891) 1983. "The Tasks of the Social Democrats in the Struggle against the Famine in Russia." In *Marxism in Russia: Key Documents 1879–1906*, edited by Neil Harding, 100–107. Cambridge: Cambridge University Press.

Polese, Abel, Thomas Ambrosio, and Tanel Kerikmäe. 2020. "Estonian Identity Construction between Nation Branding and Building." *Mezinárodni Vztahy: Czech Journal of International Relations* 55 (2): 24–46.

Pomerantsev, Peter. 2019. *This Is Not Propaganda: Adventures in the War against Reality*. London: Faber and Faber.

Potter, Simon J. 2012. *Broadcasting Empire: The BBC and the British World 1922–1970*. Oxford: Oxford University Press.

Pötzsch, Holger. 2013. "The Emergence of iWar: Changing Practices and Perceptions of Military Engagement in a Digital Era." *New Media & Society* 17 (1): 78–95.

Price, Monroe. 2015. *Free Expression, Globalism and the New Strategic Communication*. New York: Cambridge University Press.

Propp, Vladimir. (1928) 1968. *Morphology of the Folktale*. 2nd rev. ed. Bloomington: Indiana University Press.

Radio Free Europe. 2014. "Ukraine Opposition Vows to Continue Struggle after Yanukovych Offer." http://www.rferl.org/content/protesters-police-tense -standoff-ukraine/25241945.html.

Radway, Janice. (1984) 1991. *Reading the Romance: Women, Patriarchy, and Popular Literature*. Chapel Hill: University of North Carolina Press.

Radway, Janice. 1989. "Ethnography among Elites: Comparing Discourses of Power." *Journal of Communication Inquiry* 13 (2): 3–12.

Rantapelkonen, Jari, and Mirva Salminen, eds. 2013. *The Fog of Cyber Defence*. Helsinki: National Defense University.

Raykoff, Ivan, and Robert Deam Tobin, eds. 2007. *A Song for Europe: Popular Music and Politics in the Eurovision Song Contest*. London: Ashgate.

Reid, Anna. 1997. *Borderland: A Journey through the History of Ukraine*. London: Weidenfeld and Nicolson.

Reith, John. 1924. *Broadcast over Britain*. London: Hodder and Stoughton.

Renz, Bettina. 2016. "Russia and 'Hybrid Warfare.'" *Contemporary Politics* 22 (3): 283–300.

Repnikova, Maria. 2022. *Chinese Soft Power*. Cambridge: Cambridge University Press.

Rivoal, Isabelle, and Noel B. Salazar. 2013. "Contemporary Ethnographic Practice and the Value of Serendipity." *Social Anthropology* 21 (2): 178–185.

Roberts, Geoffrey. 2006. "History, Theory and the Narrative Turn in IR." *Review of International Studies* 32 (4): 703–714.

Robinson, Matt, and Pavel Polityuk. 2013. "Hedging their Bets, Ukraine's Oligarchs Sit above the Fray." Reuters, 5 December. www.reuters.com/article/uk -ukraine-oligarchs-idUKBRE9B40MQ20131205.

Roche, Maurice. 2002. *Megaevents and Modernity: Olympics and Expos in the Growth of Global Culture*. London: Routledge.

Roselle, Laura, Alister Miskimmon, and Ben O'Loughlin. 2014. "Strategic Narrative: A New Means to Understanding Soft Power." *Media, War & Conflict* 7 (1): 70–84.

Ross, Sven. 2008. *Klasstolkningar. En receptionsanalys av hur klassaspekter uppfattas i Tre kärlekar, Falcon Crest och TV–nyheter*. Stockholm: Stockholm University/JMK.

Rossiter, Ned. 2006. *Organized Networks: Media Theory, Creative Labour, New Institutions*. Rotterdam: NAi Publishers.

Roth, Andrew. 2021. "Ukraine's Football Kit with Map Featuring Crimea Causes Outrage in Russia." *Guardian*, 7 June. https://www.theguardian.com/world/2021 /jun/07/ukraine-new-football-kit-russia-national-team-shirt-annexed-crimea.

Roy, Ishita S. 2007. "Worlds Apart: Nation-Branding on the National Geographic Channel." *Media, Culture & Society* 29 (4): 569–592.

Ryabinska, Natalya. 2011. "The Media Market and Media Ownership in Post-Communist Ukraine: Impact on Media Independence and Pluralism." *Problems of Post-Communism* 58 (6): 3–20.

Ryan, Johny. 2007. "'iWar': A New Threat, Its Convenience, and Our Increasing Vulnerability." *NATO Review* 4.

Schleifer, Ron. 2012. "The Enemy's Image: Propaganda in the Arab-Israeli Conflict." In *Enemy Images in War Propaganda*, edited by Marja Vuorinen, 107–126. Newcastle upon Tyne, UK: Cambridge Scholars Publishing.

Schoenborn, Dennis. 2013. "The Pervasive Power of PowerPoint: How a Genre of Professional Communication Permeates Organizational Communication." *Organization Studies* 34 (12): 1777–1801.

Schrøder, Kim Christian. 2000. "Making Sense of Audience Discourses: Towards a Multidimensional Model of Mass Media Reception." *European Journal of Cultural Studies* 3 (2): 233–258.

Schudson, Michael. 1982. "The Politics of Narrative Form: The Emergence of News Conventions in Print and Television." *Daedalus* 111 (4): 97–112.

Schudson, Michael. 1994. "Question Authority: A History of the News Interview in American Journalism, 1860s–1930s." *Media, Culture & Society* 16:565–587.

Schudson, Michael. 2005. "News as Stories." In *Media Anthropology*, edited by Eric W. Rothenbuhler and Mihai Coman, 121–128. Thousand Oaks, CA: Sage.

Schutz, Alfred. (1932) 1980. *The Phenomenology of the Social World*. London: Heinemann Educational Books.

Searle, John. 1969. *Speech Acts: An Essay in the Philosophy of Language*. Cambridge: Cambridge University Press.

Soules, Marshall. 2015. *Media, Persuasion and Propaganda*. Edinburgh: Edinburgh University Press.

Sparks, Colin. 1998. *Communism, Capitalism and the Mass Media*. London: Sage.

Stade, Ronald. 2017. "Introduction: The Social Life of Contentious Concepts." *Conflict and Society* 3 (1): 73–77.

Ståhlberg, Per. 2017. "Från marknadsföring till propagandakrig." *Ikaros, tidskrift om människan och vetenskapen* 2:37–39.

Ståhlberg, Per, and Göran Bolin. 2015. "Nationen som vara och gemenskap: Identitet, agens och publik i nationsmarknadsföring." *Nordisk Østforum* 29 (3): 289–312.

Ståhlberg, Per, and Göran Bolin. 2016. "Having a Soul or Choosing a Face? Nation Branding, Identity and Cosmopolitan Imagination." *Social Identities* 22 (3): 274–290.

Stark, David, and Verena Paravel. 2008. "PowerPoint in Public: Digital Technologies and the Morphology of Demonstration." *Theory, Culture & Society* 25 (5): 30–55.

Stepinska, Agnieszka. 2010. "9/11 and the Transformation of Globalized Media Events." In *Media Events in a Global Age*, edited by Nick Couldry, Andreas Hepp, and Friedrich Krotz, 203–213. London: Routledge.

Stepnisky, Jeffrey. 2020. "Staging Atmosphere on the Ukrainian Maidan." *Space and Culture* 23 (2): 80–97.

Stolyarchuk, Bozhena. 2013. "A Brandless Country." *Kyiv Weekly* 18:3.

Strömbäck, Jesper. 2008. "Four Phases of Mediatization: An Analysis of the Mediatization of Politics." *International Journal of Press/Politics* 133:228–246.

Sukhov, Oleg. 2015. "Protesting Putin: Kremlin Starts Two-War Strategy in Syria, Ukraine." *Kyiv Post*, 1 October. http://www.kyivpost.com/content/ukraine/protesting-putin-kremlin-starts-two-war-strategy-in-syria-ukraine-399117.html.

Surowiec, Pawel. 2016. *Nation Branding, Public Relations and Soft Power*. London: Routledge.

Surowiec, Pawel. 2017. "Post-Truth Soft Power: Changing Facets of Propaganda, Kompromat, and Democracy." *Georgetown Journal of International Affairs* 18 (3): 21–27.

Surowiec, Pawel, and Ilan Manor, eds. 2021. *Public Diplomacy and the Politics of Uncertainty*. Cham, Switzerland: Palgrave Macmillan.

Sveriges Television. 2013. "Det liknar en revolution." *SVT Nyheter*, 1 December. https://www.svt.se/nyheter/utrikes/hundratusentals-protesterar-i-kiev.

Szostek, Joanna. 2014. "The Media Battles of Ukraine's EuroMaidan." *Digital Icons: Studies in Russian, Eurasian and Central European New Media* 11:1–19.

Szostek, Joanna. 2018. "News Media Repertoires and Strategic Narrative Reception: A Paradox of Dis/belief in Authoritarian Russia." *New Media & Society* 20 (1): 68–87.

Taylor, Charles. 2002. "Modern Social Imaginaries." *Public Culture* 14 (1): 91–124.

The Telegraph. 2016. "Eurovision 2016: Furious Russia Demands Boycott of Ukraine over Jamala's 'Anti-Kremlin' Song." 16 May. https://www.telegraph.co.uk/news/2016/05/15/eurovision-2016-furious-russia-demands-boycott-of-ukraine-over-j/.

Thomas, William I., and Dorothy S. Thomas. 1928. *The Child in America: Behavior Problems and Programs*. New York: A. A. Knopf.

Todorov, Tzvetan. 1969. "Structural Analysis of Narrative." *Novel: A Forum of Fiction* 3 (1): 70–76.

Törnquist-Plewa, Barbara, and Yuliya Yurchuk. 2019. "Memory Politics in Contemporary Ukraine: Reflections from the Postcolonial Perspective." *Memory Studies* 12 (6): 699–720.

Tribe, Laurence H. 1985. "Constitutional Calculus: Equal Justice or Economic Efficiency?" *Harvard Law Review* 98 (3): 592–621.

Tsybulska, Liubov. 2020. "Ukraine Uncovers Russian Propaganda: Will the Center for Countering Disinformation Succeed?" Ukraine Crisis Media Center, 3 November. https://uacrisis.org/en/tsentr-iz-protydiyi-dezinformatsiyi.

Tufte, Edward R. 2003. *The Cognitive Style of PowerPoint*. Cheshire, CT: Graphics Press.

Tumber, Howard, and Frank Webster. 2006. *Journalists under Fire: Information War and Journalistic Practices*. London: Sage.

Turner, Victor, and Edith Turner. 1978. *Image and Pilgrimage in Christian Culture: Anthropological Perspectives*. New York: Columbia University Press.

Ukraine Crisis Media Center. 2017. "What Hindered the Coloring of a Soviet Monument into a Rainbow in Kyiv." 2 May. https://uacrisis.org/en/55918-soviet-monument-rainbow.

Umland, Andreas. 2019. "Irregular Militias and Radical Nationalism in Post-Euromaydan Ukraine: The Prehistory and Emergence of the 'Azov' Battalion in 2014." *Terrorism and Political Violence* 31 (1): 105–131.

Umland, Andreas, and Anton Shekhovtsov. 2014. "Ukraininskie pravye radikaly, evrointegratsiya i neofashistskaya ugroza." Polit.ru, 21 May. http://polit.ru/article/2014/05/21/ukraine/.

van Dijck, José, Thomas Poell, and Martijn de Waal. 2018. *The Platform Society: Public Values in a Connected World*. Oxford: Oxford University Press.

van Gennep, Arnold. 1909. *The Rites of Passage*. London: Routledge and Kegan Paul.

Van Ham, Peter. 2001. "The Rise of the Brand State: The Postmodern Politics of Image and Reputation." *Foreign Affairs*, 2–6.

Ventsel, Andreas, Sten Hansson, Mari-Liis Madisson, and Vladimir Sazonov. 2021. "Discourse of Fear in Strategic Narratives: The Case of Russia's Zapad War Games." *Media, War & Conflict* 14 (1): 21–39.

Verón, Eliseo. 2014. "Mediatization Theory: A Semio-Anthropological Approach." In *Mediatization of Communication*, edited by Knut Lundby, 163–172. Berlin: De Gruyter.

Volcic, Zala. 2008. "Former Yugoslavia on the World Wide Web: Commercialization and the Branding of Nation-states." *International Communication Gazette* 70 (5): 395–413.

Volcic, Zala. 2012. "Branding Slovenia: 'You Can't Spell Slovenia without Love.'" In *Branding Post-Communist Nations: Marketizing National Identities in the "New" Europe*, edited by Nadia Kaneva, 147–167. New York: Routledge.

Volcic, Zala, and Mark Andrejevic. 2011. "Nation Branding in the Era of Commercial Nationalism." *International Journal of Communication* 5:598–618.

Voronova, Liudmila. 2017. "Gender Politics of the 'War of Narratives': Russian TV News in the Times of Conflict in Ukraine." *Catalan Journal of Communication and Cultural Studies* 9 (2): 217–235.

Voronova, Liudmila. 2020. "Between Dialogue and Confrontation: Two Countries—One Profession Project and the Split in Ukrainian Journalism Culture." *Central European Journal of Communication* 13 (1): 24–30.

Voronova, Liudmila, and Andreas Widholm. 2019. "Broadcasting against the Grain: The Contradictory Roles of RT in a Global Media Age." In *Transnational Media: Concepts and Cases*, edited by Suman Mishra and Rebecca Kern-Stone, 207–213. Hoboken, NJ: John Wiley and Sons.

Vuletic, Dean. 2018. *Postwar Europe and the Eurovision Song Contest*. London: Bloomsbury Publishing.

Vuorinen, Marja, ed. 2012. *Enemy Images in War Propaganda*. Newcastle upon Tyne, UK: Cambridge Scholars Publishing.

Wagnsson, Charlotte, and Costan Barzanje. 2021. "A Framework for Analysing Antagonistic Narrative Strategies: A Russian Tale of Swedish Decline." *Media, War & Conflict* 14 (2): 239–257.

Walker, Vivian S. 2015. *State Narratives in Complex Media Environments: The Case of Ukraine*. Case 331. Washington, DC: Institute for the Study of Diplomacy, Georgetown University.

Wallace, Anthony. 1966. *Religion: An Anthropological View*. New York: Random House.

Wikicitynomika. 2014. *Guiding Principles of Ukrainian Tourism Brand*. Kyiv: National Agency for Tourism and Resorts. http://prohotelia.com/wp-content/uploads/2014/03/ukraine_tourist_brand_brandbook.pdf.

Wilkinson, Cai. 2014. "Putting 'Traditional Values' into Practice: The Rise and Contestation of Anti-Homo Propaganda Laws in Russia." *Journal of Human Rights* 13 (3): 363–379.

Williams, Raymond. (1958) 1963. *Culture and Society 1780–1950*. Harmondsworth, UK: Penguin.

Williams, Raymond. 1976. *Keywords: A Vocabulary of Culture and Society*. London: Fontana.

Wolczuk, Kataryna. 2000. "History, Europe and the 'National Idea': The 'Official' Narrative of National Identity in Ukraine." *Nationalities Papers* 28 (4): 671–694.

Woolley, Samuel C., and Philip N. Howard. 2019. "Introduction: Computational Propaganda Worldwide." In *Computational Propaganda: Political Parties, Politicians, and Political Manipulation on Social Media*, edited by Samuel C. Woolley and Philip N. Howard, 3–20. Oxford: Oxford University Press.

Wright, Charles R. 1959. *Mass Communication: A Sociological Perspective*. New York: Random House.

Yablokov, Ilya. 2015. "Conspiracy Theories as a Russian Public Diplomacy Tool: The Case of Russia Today (RT)." *Politics* 35 (4): 301–315.

Yablokov, Ilya, and Precious Chatterjee-Doody. 2022. *Russia Today and Conspiracy Theories: People, Power and Politics on RT*. London: Routledge.

Yates, JoAnne, and Wanda Orlikowski. 2007. "The PowerPoint Presentation and Its Corollaries: How Genres Shape Communicative Action in Organisations."

In *Communicative Practices in Workplaces and the Professions: Cultural Perspectives on the Regulation of Discourse and Organisations*, edited by Mark Zachry and Charlotte Thralls, 67–92. Amityville, NY: Baywood Publishing.

Yekechyk, Serhy. 2015. *The Conflict in Ukraine: What Everyone Needs to Know*. Oxford: Oxford University Press.

Yurchuk, Yuliya. 2021. "Historians as Activists: History-Writing in Times of War; the Case of Ukraine in 2014–2018." *Nationalities Papers* 49 (4): 691–709.

INDEX

Information Policy Series

Edited by Sandra Braman